"I Only Want What's Best For You"

"I Only Want What's Best For You"

A Parent's Guide to Raising Well-Adjusted Children

Judith R. Brown, Ph.D.

CEDAR

An imprint of William Heinemann Ltd

Published by Cedar Books
an imprint of William Heinemann Ltd.
10 Upper Grosvenor Street, London W1X 9PA

LONDON MELBOURNE
JOHANNESBURG AUCKLAND

Published 1986 by St Martin's Press, New York
First published in Great Britain 1987 by The Kingwood Press
First Cedar edition 1987

Design by Giorgetta Bell McRee

0 434 11137 6

Printed in Great Britain by
Richard Clay Ltd,
Bungay, Suffolk

*To my mother, Eva Simon Winer, and
to the memory of my father, Harry Winer,
who created a happy environment for me—
inside the family.*

And especially to my husband, George.

Contents

Introduction

During the years I was bringing children into the world, I took my family and all families for granted. I grew up in one. Everyone I knew lived in one. Families were. It was that simple. What more was there to say? Thirty-five years ago I had ideas about what kind of parent was a "good" one. I knew certain things I never wanted to do with my children, like spank them on the street, as I had seen other mothers—"bad" mothers—do. I read a book about childbirth before my first child was born. What did I know about being a parent? What was there to know?

Now my young friends are having children. Their husbands know more about having a baby than I knew! Young parents seem to have a world of information about birthing, bonding, and bringing up their babies. They are aware of emotional as well as physical require-ments for the growing and developing child. They, like preceding generations, want what is best for their children.

The paradox is that at the very moment we want what is best for our children, we unwittingly create relationships that disrupt their well-being. Perhaps a greater paradox is that no matter how much we learn about being a parent from books or courses, the parenting we got as infants and children is the indelible lesson that will not be readily erased. The seeds planted in our own early years of development may lie dormant over a long period. Then, when we have our own children, we discover emotions that disturb us, feelings that threaten us, and actions we do not recognize as coming from the person we thought we were. All are apparently unearthed by the existence of our children. This "dark side" or "shadow," which we have kept a secret from ourselves, is no secret to our children.

Carl Jung has written that the most direct way of avoiding our own shadow is by "looking for everything dark, inferior, and culpable in *others*." Our partners and our children become the "others" in our lives. The stage is created for playing out what I call innocent evil inside our families. Parents who need to imagine themselves as always right and blameless avoid their shadow by finding their children wrong and to blame. Children thus used are so busy being faulty for their parents, they never have a chance to become themselves. Even as adults, long after *they* are parents and their parents are dead, they feel basically wrong and at fault.

Parents' emotional needs can easily eclipse their children's needs, for the dependent child does what seems necessary to avoid losing Mother and Father. Many of us had to put our parents' needs first when we were young. In an attempt to gain the acceptance and support we all require as infants and children, we become, to some degree, frauds, trying to be what we are not—perfect. As adults we still live under the curse of perfectionism and wonder why we wake up depressed, emotionally paralyzed, with life's juices barely trickling. Some people spend their lives searching for their true self, their real identity, which was nipped in the bud way back when.

In the stylized world of Chinese opera, evil is portrayed by distortion; the essence of evil is expressed in the twisted feature, the disproportioned limb. So in the family is evil manifested in distortion: the relationships that go awry, the love that becomes pain, the young lives that end up askew.

My children are adults now. We have all grown. For twenty years I have been a psychotherapist working with individuals, couples, and families, as well as a trainer of psychotherapists. My goal now is to take some of the light that professionals have shed on what families are all about, adding what I have gleaned in my years with my own family and what I have learned in my years working with others, and to direct this light out to other parents who ask themselves the questions that I have asked: Is it worth it? Will we all survive? And especially, what is going on in our family?

I hope this book provides a fresh perspective, an impetus to try some alternatives that may enable you to find more gratification, fulfillment, and joy within your family.

How, having killed our own people,
should we be happy?

—BHAGAVAD GITA

"I Only Want What's Best For You"

1 | Parenting in Perspective

A mother, embracing her young daughter, kisses her hard on the cheek. The little girl says, "Mommy, you're hurting me." Mother responds, "No, dear, Mommy loves you."

This seems a rather benign example of parental abuse. Compared to the harsh forms of physical abuse that can be perpetrated against youngsters it appears subtle and nonviolent. This mother may actually be carried away with affection for her child. She may sincerely love the child, and perhaps not know her own strength. Yet what comes across in this simple scene is how the mother looks after her own interests rather than respond to her child: she does not acknowledge that she is hurting her child; she contradicts her child's words and nullifies the child's experience. Mother's prevailing need is to perpetuate an ideal view of herself: I am a mother who loves my child and would never hurt her.

The boy in the following episode is nine years old. His family has been in a therapy session for an hour. He seems bored, uninterested in what is going on. He stands by his mother's chair playing with the window shade. Father says, "Stop that." Mother says, in an exasperated voice, "Why are you doing that? Do you want attention?" The boy, catching his mother's tone of voice, which implies, "You'd better not want attention," answers, "No." "Yes, you do," contradicts his mother. Out of self-interest this woman, like the other, flatly denies her child's experience. She is in the stressful situation of a family therapy session with her husband and three youngsters. Above all she wants to keep her level of stress bearable. Her son pesters her. She quickly construes the situation in a way that is less threatening for her. Her son is wrong, wrong, wrong, and she silences him consummately.

A common assumption is that parents look out for their children's interests. Otherwise the state, which looks out for those who cannot look out for themselves, would provide advocates for children of parents whose first concern is consistently themselves. But what happens when the parents' interests come first? We have Hansel and Gretel and Snow White, in the well-known folktales. In real life when parents misinterpret their own interests as their children's we have scenes like this. A mother, after a brief altercation with her three-year-old son, coaxes him to her, "Come, give me a kiss. You love Mommy?" After numerous experiences of this kind he acquires a skewed idea of giving and receiving love. This orientation brings him little satisfaction in later years with his assorted wives. Another child receives a gift from a visitor, eagerly opens the package, but before she can explore and discover in her own way, Father says, "This is the right way to hold it. Here, let me show you." This girl learns, after years of "Let me show you . . .," to be extremely cautious, afraid to try anything new. Her view of herself as an adult is "I can't do anything right."

The following was the experience of a friend:

> My mother always told me how bad men are. She even kept me from my father. Well, my father pretty much ignored me, anyway, and my mother encouraged it. Then, when I got older, she kept after me: 'Why don't you find yourself a nice man?'"

We are horrified at the thought of physically abusing or harming our children in any way. We put ourselves in a different category from those who do; *we* are conscientious and caring parents. *We* have our children's interests at heart and we would never replay under our roofs either the folktale plots nor such scenes as those related above. We take our job as parents seriously, perhaps as the greatest challenge we have yet faced. But every day on your street and mine parents are putting their emotional and psychological interests before those of their children. Chances are, they are never aware of it. They are parents like you and like me.

The critical factor seems to be pretense. Our children become our victims when we parents hide from ourselves, when we don't experience who we are and what we do, when we give altruistic reasons to explain our actions. The most common reason given is: we want what is best for our children. Parents who are unwilling or incapable of confronting themselves, their inner wishes and needs, live behind a mask of distortion; they exist in an illusion. To paraphrase Laurens Van der Post in *Jung and the Story of Our Time*, it is parents' lack of knowledge of themselves and their motives that calls up disaster. A close relationship with someone who has blinders on is a dangerous undertaking, as children know very well, and as you may remember from your own childhood. As a child, you must either relinquish your reality, your experience of what is, and share the parental illusions, or you become the troublemaker, unacceptable, the enemy. One man told me that he realized very early in his life that his view of people and the world differed greatly from that of his parents. He explained this to himself the way many children do. These were not his real parents. He was really a prince who was being tested. Eventually he would be called back to his true home. Meanwhile he would be a good boy and pass the test.

Any emotional use of children by parents will undermine their development. Alice Miller, a Swiss psychiatrist who has written wisely and extensively on the subject, writes in her book *Prisoners of Childhood* (published in paperback as *The Drama of the Gifted Child*): "As soon as the child is regarded as a possession for which one has a particular goal, as soon as one exerts control over him, his vital growth will be violently interrupted." She maintains that it is a child's legitimate "need to be regarded and respected as the person he really is at any given time, and as the center—the central actor—in his own activity." For children needed as a supporting chorus, the parents' story clearly outranks their own.

We use our children as our possessions when we focus our own needs on them. Here, as an example, is a woman who needed the mothering she didn't get from her own mother. She groomed her daughter for this role. The daughter tells how she felt responsible for her mother's well-being since "before I could remember." She went on a week's cruise with her elderly mother, convinced that she had finally graduated from being her mother's keeper. Every day her mother drank cup after cup of coffee right up to bedtime, then started each morning complaining how poorly she had slept. After her breakfast of sausages and bacon, she would spend the hours until lunch talking of her upset stomach. The woman reported it took every bit of self-control to refrain from taking up her habitual caretaking. After all, she had played that role since early childhood. Inside, however, she was screaming, "But, Mother, if you didn't drink so much coffee . . ."

A father uses his child as his possession when his ambition for his son is overlaid on the boy's interests and talents. "Art is not a profession! You must be a physician." At forty-eight the doctor son is deep in a mid-life crisis. His days feel empty, his wife complains that he acts like an old man. Twenty years married to work while his heart was elsewhere has taken its toll.

We perpetrate our innocent evil when we attempt to become the constant directors of our children's experience, when we "know what is best for them," not only in how to use the new toy the "right" way, but what, when, and how to feel and express themselves. We encase them in a veneer that reflects our needs and our shadows, prompting them to conceal from the world, and eventually from themselves, who and how they truly are. We minimize their sense of self; we disqualify the validity of their experiences, we disqualify them. This brand of evil is innocent in the sense that it is carried out without conscious intention by parents who want only what is best for their children. It is often the case that parents make a deliberate effort to provide their child with quality experiences in all areas of life. Unfortunately their deliberate effort is often in opposition to their unacknowledged inner wishes and needs, and therefore must result in an outcome that is awry in some profound sense.

The literature about evil, from the earliest times to the present, is full of quotations that equate evil with denial, with false beliefs regarding one's own nature, with ignorance and unawareness. In regard to families, parents do have powerful needs. These are disguised and ignored, but they emerge to distort the life of the child.

Reality is sometimes hard to face; we weave more agreeable fantasies in its place. Fairytale substitutions are easier to live with than a past that is unpleasant or downright fearful, or a present that clashes with our self-concept. Perhaps at some time you looked at other parents with their children and wondered, "Can't they see what they're doing?" Probably they can't see. (Someone has described the family as "the ties that blind.") In our dealings with family members we superimpose over reality our personal myths, those that we have accepted from our parents and those we have created for ourselves.

The real danger for our children lies in what is hidden behind our mythology. Well-intentioned we may be, striving to be successful in this most important challenge of bringing up children, yet as long as we are blind to the reality of ourselves and our interaction with our children, we are living an illusion. As children discover, trying to interact with an illusion is like attempting to catch hold of a rainbow. Impossible. They can't get through the wall of the parents' interests and get hold of a true response; they gradually lose touch with their own experience as well, since to voice their reality is a threat to their parents' illusion. They will always lose, for a child's sense of wholeness depends on the parents' integrity.

The most common self-deception of parents is that what they do in relation to their children, regardless of how self-gratifying it may be, is basically *for* the children.

Becoming and being a parent has been described in glowing terms by mothers and fathers who credit parenthood with giving them everything from a "new view of the universe" to a "new lease on life." How did we ever get along B.C.—before children—when our house was empty of baby furniture, our floor clear of toys, before chubby arms wrapped around our neck, and the irresistible smile wrapped around our heart? There's no doubt that as parents we have countless opportunities to be more, to be better, finer people than we knew we could be; and to enjoy inherent satisfactions we didn't know possible.

Notwithstanding all that we get out of being with and doing for our children—parenting, that is—nurturing and rearing our young are primarily for them. They are born totally dependent, needing constant care. Basically, what do they need? The young need shelter, food, stimulation, and connection with others. These ensure physical health and growth. They need people who caress and make comforting sounds, whose attitude assures them, "We want you, we love you, you belong to us, and we know how to care for you." Thus children acquire the freedom to develop and flourish.

They also need authority, which guides and prepares them to live in the world of the family and in the larger worlds of school and community. All this guidance, all these ministrations and admonitions result in the child's ability to achieve adulthood, to pack up his favorite records and posters, step over the threshold into independence, and experience a rich, full life. In a nutshell, that's what we needed from our parents and that's what our kids need from us.

Parents can, and do, derive pleasure from caring for, training, and guiding their children, which is a good thing, considering how exhausting, frustrating, and relentless children can be. Yet deriving pleasure is not the same as trying to fill the insufficiencies in our own lives. A mother who says as she shows off her baby to a friend, "Now I'll never be alone again," already has the child in fetters. When parents find a child useful to save a marriage, or to try to fill an insatiable craving for affection, or to attain what was unattainable for themselves, then the parenting is no longer primarily for the child. No matter how pristine our intentions, how intelligent our approaches, if our parenting is coming through underground channels of our needs, it is inevitable that it will come out contaminated.

It is not easy to find a clear line that separates actions primarily for the child and those that are distorted into being overwhelmingly for the parent. We're talking about intangibles. How much? How long? With what attitude? In what context?

The example of a mother breast-feeding her child is a good illustration of the difficulty in categorizing any parental action as "primarily" for the child or for the parent. Like much parenting, it is not exclusively for one or the other, but serves each in different ways. Physically the mother needs the baby to relieve her breasts of the milk. For some weeks after the birth she profits from the effects on her uterus. These are real, experienced, *physical* benefits. At the same time a mother may achieve *emotional* advantages. She feels the profound connection between her and her baby when the little one cries and her milk begins to flow. "It's a thrilling experience!" "I feel so close to my baby." "I get the satisfaction of knowing I'm doing the best for my baby." "If my mother could do it, so can I." As joyous as the act of nursing may be for the mother, as satisfying and fulfilling, its prime purpose is nourishment for the child.

Under some conditions the scale gets tipped and nursing appears to be primarily for the mother. A single mother nurses her five-year-old daughter every morning and night. Does the child need this or does the mother need this? In her book *Song of Solomon*, Toni Morrison has a chilling scene of a mother nursing her son at her breast in a special room of her house: "She sat in this room holding her son on her lap, staring at his closed eyelids and listening to the sound of his sucking. Staring not so much from maternal joy as from a wish to avoid seeing his legs dangling almost to the floor."

Under the guise of parenting, mothers and fathers

may try to fill the empty places in their existence. In the above example, I think we can safely say that the scales have been tipped. The nursing is no longer nourishment for the child, who, by the description, is old enough to go to the refrigerator, get a glass of milk, and make himself a cheese sandwich. The nourishment is for the mother. The author says that this "secret indulgence" was what got the mother through the day. The significance of the special room is that it had been her father's, to whom she was more than a daughter. Now her father was dead, and her son "came reluctantly, as a chore, and lay as he had at least once each day of his life in his mother's arms. . . ." The distorted relationship of the woman and her father was re-created between the woman and her child. She attempted to establish the love and closeness she had previously had from her father with her son. The act of nursing, of mothering, was a pretense for the mother to appease her own hunger.

A mother's body has a place for the new life to grow, protected, for the first nine months. That's obviously essential for the child. The mother reaps some benefits, too; some women more, some fewer. There are feelings of fulfillment: to produce the next generation, after all, is a natural function of the female body. The reality of the baby comes to the mother with added excitement when she feels movement: there is truly a living being developing; in a few months she'll hold a real child, *their* child, in her arms. It seems that no matter how great an importance the mother gives to her pregnant condition, nature's arrangement is overwhelmingly for the child. We know that the baby will get what it needs for nourishment from the mother's body, even to the possible detriment of the mother's physical state.

Yet there are mothers who, out of their own emotional starvation and vulnerability, take the pregnancy as nourishment and protection primarily for themselves. A young mother relates, "When I got pregnant I began to feel important for the first time in my life." Another mother says, "I knew as soon as he heard I was expecting that he wouldn't leave." One mother told her daughter, "I wanted you in my life to do something for me. You were supposed to keep your father here. When you didn't do that, I didn't know what to do with you."

From the moment the newborn makes eye contact with the parent, it is impossible to say the parent gets this much and the child gets that much out of the experience. Absurd to try. And when that sweet-smelling little body, wrapped in the after-bath towel, is cuddled in the parent's arms, who gets the most out of it? It is truly satisfying for both. The interaction of diaper changing, bedtimes, and habitually shared life under one roof generally fosters the growth of feelings of acceptance, attachment, and belonging. Many parents have problems around such issues themselves. In some cases they missed out on authentic, caring parenting. It is in these areas of being accepted, closely connected to another person, and belonging that parents, eager to get what they need, may lose sight of the child. Then, instead of parenting to provide what the child needs, they groom the child to provide what they, the parents, need.

All parent/child interaction answers the attachment, acceptance, and belonging needs of parent and child to some degree. We are gregarious. We need people to respond to and to respond to us. What we share seems secondary to the sharing itself; we need the interchange. When it came to thinking of the worst punishment for others, it was logical that someone came up with solitary confinement. A mother and young child are so close to one another as they share much of the daily routine that one's enjoyment becomes the other's, and one's discomfort becomes the other's.

A mother might enjoy the company of her child or not, may need it desperately or not. But, for the child, interaction with another is absolutely essential. It seems that a child will strike any bargain necessary to ensure a steady supply of contact, especially from that most important person, a parent (usually the mother). Like the boy who went reluctantly to nurse daily at his mother's breast, children will reluctantly brush Mother's hair, sit on Daddy's lap, or give up friends of their own age in order to keep their lifeline intact.

It is natural that as a child grows toward more and more autonomy, his or her dependence on the parents gradually lessens. Often it is the parents who have trouble letting go, as many nursery school teachers can attest. They see mothers literally clinging to children, unable to accept that their youngsters are quite ready to join the others with only a casual wave of dismissal in their direction.

Tom, an eighteen-year-old, was concerned about his divorced mother. Ever since he could remember she had told him, "You're all I have." Could he ever leave home? Tom questioned whether he was using his mother as an excuse to stay home. Did he really have the gumption to get out on his own? He was afraid he'd never leave the comforts to which he was so accustomed and the companionship of his mother. And he was all she had. When a parent needs attachment as much as, or more than, the child, both of them are in trouble. It doesn't take long before the child senses the parent's needs and does what is necessary to protect the parent's interests.

In his book *Infants and Mothers*, Dr. T. Berry Brazelton, an authority on infants and child care, includes a description of Laura. When Laura was only a few months old she had picked up on the fact that her parents needed to hover over her. How does a child so young become aware of parents' needs? It is truly a marvel—and a mystery. At eight months she was a helpless kind of "puffball," keeping her parents busy fetching and carrying for her. One day her mother was sick in bed and her father spent a good deal of time taking care of his wife. What a surprise when they found out Laura was perfectly capable of moving herself around, reaching her toys, and even inching herself along the floor on her stomach, into the parents' bedroom when they left her alone!

Children will turn into a bundle of demands for a mother who needs to be harried, a clinging vine with school phobia for a mother who needs the child at home, or any of a variety of less than fully developed people for parents whose needs for attachment take precedence over their children's needs to grow and develop. Mothers especially, since they are almost always the parent who takes primary care of the infant and very young child, are in the position to rejoice with the child and stimulate each new ability. Or, if they are vulnerable and threatened by the child's growth, mothers are there to discourage what will eventually take the child from them: the child's growing independence.

We all know that parents' acceptance is vital to a child. Some of us as adults still do emotional cartwheels trying to get it or to get free from needing it. As Elizabeth Keeler wrote in her poem "A Daughter's Funeral Dirge at a Saturday Burial":

> *She is dead and all the waiting*
> *for the glass of her thanksgiving*
> *proves a waiting at the table*
> *where wine isn't served.*

> *All my war to make her happy*
> *she has clearly won by dying.*

Attachment, acceptance, and belonging are all interwoven. A child forms healthy attachments to parents when there are feelings of acceptance and belonging. They all can be turned topsy-turvy when one or both parents see the child as a source of emotional sustenance and latches on. Then they groom their child to take care of them, a dwarf parent for the parents. You may remember:

> *James, James, Morrison, Morrison*
> *Weatherby George Dupree*
> *Took good care of his mother,*
> *Although he was only three.*

I once asked a middle-aged man to picture himself at the age of three years, and he replied, "I see myself, a little blond boy with big blue eyes, carrying my parents on my shoulders." A heavy burden.

What a lot of power showers down on the small child whose parent needs acceptance from him or her! It is easy to imagine that when a child pouts or cries, the parent feels rejected or a failure. There is only one thing for the parent to do then: try harder; be sweeter, or kinder, or more indulgent, or whatever. The parent ends up exhausted and the child becomes a tyrant. One mother remembers how threatened she felt when one of her sons challenged her with the full force of his year-and-a-half-old will to have his way. "They all had minds of their own," she says, "but somehow he was different." Now he is in his twenties, lying on the couch most of the time, alienating everyone in the family and extremely unhappy himself. His mother adds, "He walks around and his very presence says what a bad mother I was. Sometimes he even voices it; that really gets to me." He tyrannizes them with his depression. If they are not nice to him, he might commit suicide.

It is not a child's concern to approve or disapprove of parents. Parents who need their children's approval are asking for trouble. When the child wields the whip of disapproval, the parent/child power balance goes haywire.

There are parents who not only make their child their judge, but want the whole world to see that they are indeed exemplary parents. The child becomes the vehicle for the parent, and parenting has little or nothing to do with the child's needs. The child must conduct himself with an eye to "what others might think." The parent pleads with the reluctant eater: "Would you like a sandwich? How about pancakes? Eat just one bite for Mother, please. What will people say if you look like I starve you?"

Neither the parent nor the child alone determines how the interaction will develop between them. Any parent who has more than one child will tell how one child reacted one way and another child quite differently to some particular action. "Barbara always had to pick out her own clothes. From an early age she was so fussy. If I simply took clothes to put on her I'd have a fight on my hands. Jack never cared what I put on him." Another example: "When Bill was unhappy he would sit on my lap and let me calm him down. Tom would have none of that. He would put up a kind of brave front as if to say, 'I'll take care of myself. I don't need you.'"

Barbara, who wanted to choose her own clothes in the case above, did not singly determine the interaction between herself and her mother. Many a mother has taken on the battle of the wardrobe every day with such a child. In the matter of clothing Barbara's mother chose not to have a "fight on her hands," but to defer to her daughter. Together they established their interaction. Yet the child is not an equal of the parent, with the same level of responsibility for what transpires between them. The parent is at a higher level of development, intellectually, emotionally, and physically. He or she has more awareness, is not dependent on the approval of the child as the child is on the approval and goodwill of the parent.

The parent has everything that the helpless newborn and the developing child want and need: food, acceptance, protection. Infants are totally self-centered in that they are out to survive and will do whatever is necessary to get what they need. If they only get what they need when Mother is happy, they will learn to keep Mother happy, not in an altruistic way, for Mother, but in a self-serving way, to ensure their own survival.

Videos of parents and infants taken by research psychologists show how early the patterns of interaction develop. If a mother tends to respond more readily to an infant who looks downcast, the child will quickly learn this and behave accordingly. The child picks up with consummate skill what is required to get the responses he or she wants—that is, life-giving nourishment and contact.

If necessary, children will take on behavior that actually goes against their growth and development in order to please parents. We have seen how an infant played helpless. Children play stupid, give up their sanity, and sacrifice their independence. We often see children scaling one mountain after another for the parental pat on the head, one that never comes. Well known is the cliché of the parent perusing the report card, "Yes, that's pretty good, but what is that B doing among the A's?"

Children, with each day's development, become more and more capable of taking over their own lives, from holding their own bottle and spoon to going to the toilet and getting themselves to school. They become increasingly adept at expressing themselves, at complying with or refusing parental demands. For a mother who wants a child's cheerful compliance, the toddler's "No!" comes like a verbal baseball bat. Lucky are the youngsters whose parents use sensitivity and intelligence to encourage and support their personal power and autonomy, rather than being threatened by their developing independence.

A child benefits not only from physical parenting but also from the whole process of socialization, of becoming fit to live among others. The general tendency is for children to want to be acceptable. Who wants to be ostracized? Parents have something called *identification* on their side when it comes to socializing their youngsters; kids want to be like the grown-ups they admire. They copy what Mom and Dad do.

The socialization of the child benefits the parents, too. Imagine having a baby who wants to play all night and sleep all day. That simply doesn't go over very well in a household. And how can you get a baby-sitter if a five-year-old refuses to use a toilet? How can you take an obnoxious youngster to a restaurant?

Yet teaching a child to fit into the society of which he is a member can be perverted, twisted around, so that the process becomes something primarily for the parents. Kids feel it when the parents' concern is not for them but for how they reflect on the parents. One child said, "I know exactly how my parents want me to be and none of it has anything to do with me." Then what to do? Show the world what a good parent Mother or Father is by doing "the right thing" and being the "good" child? Or refuse to perform, be true to oneself, and disappoint the parent? A real bind, especially when the child knows that punishment in some form may follow. A disappointed parent isn't apt to suggest, "Come on, everybody, let's get ice cream!" A parent who feels betrayed may withhold more than ice cream.

Parents, except for rare exceptions, love to see their children succeed. Just look at the faces in the audience bursting with pride at any school function. They make sacrifices of time and money, they chauffeur miles a week for lessons, they supervise practice sessions and homework by the hour. The children blossom under this special care, and the parents wear the feather of their child's success in their cap proudly. But if all the chauffeuring, and the practicing, and the homework sessions are first and foremost to ensure a feather in Mom's or Dad's cap, then parents and child are all apt to end up disappointed. The parents' love and approval get bound up in the child's being outstanding. The need to please turns the child into a show-off, and the inherent satisfaction in excelling is lost.

Children sense the difference between parents whose concern is for them and parents whose concern is primarily narcissistic. Yet children accommodate to parents' psychological and physical needs. They have to; they really have no choice in the matter. Children's needs are basic survival needs. Their total dependence on their parents and their hunger for validation make them sensitive to how they must be and what they must do in relation to their parents.

As the iceberg that shows above the water is merely the tip, so the interaction between parent and child that we see and hear is but a small part of what passes between them. In our anxiety to be good parents and do what is right for our children, we tend to focus on the surface, seeking ways to be that we think will ensure happy, healthy children. A young woman who decided to see a therapist for a few sessions told me what happened when she told her parents of that decision. They became very agitated, saying, "We love you, we love you." Throughout her childhood they had totally ignored what transpired between them and their daughter below the surface, the level that is most powerful. In ignoring what is not readily apparent we parents often miss the essential point: "Are my secret interests elbowing their way into first place? What do I, the parent, need, and how do I attempt to get it through my child?"

2 | How Parents' Needs Involve Children

Any parent who has had difficulty in getting a child to submit to making a bed or putting food back in the refrigerator when lunch is over may be astonished at the emotional hook-ins whereby a child, without protest, seems ready to sacrifice his or her very existence to gratify a parent's emotional needs. How does a parent get a kid to do that? The answer is that what is secret, and therefore covert, is frightfully potent. The power of the parent's unconscious far surpasses any of the obvious interactions that we are all aware of in our families. If, as a parent, you have undetected subterranean fears waiting to be stirred, fears that you need to keep out of your awareness, your child will be affected. A youngster may not intuit the nature of these fears, but he or she certainly picks up when you become agitated, when your breath quickens and your face hardens, or you leave the room to take a pill.

Frances Wickes's *The Inner World of Childhood* has many examples of children who carry the outer symptoms of a parent's hidden fear. In one case a boy was perceived as retarded by his mother. The woman had carried a heavy load of guilt in regard to her own retarded brother. As a child she had been ashamed of him and glad when he died at fifteen. She had believed that should she ever get married and have children she would surely have a son who would repeat his tragic story. Her unrelieved guilt and her secret fears of punishment were never spoken of; she did not acknowledge even to herself that she carried this burden. Yet her own son developed exactly as she had feared. He acted, he even tested, as a retarded child and was only saved from continuing on that mistaken path by a knowledgeable and sensitive therapist (Wickes) who met the boy when he was nine years old. The mother, impelled by her need to re-create an unfinished situation in her own life, was raising her son to fit her script. The so-called retarded child later became a distinguished doctor.

This extreme example gives us an idea how strong is the influence of the fragmented, unfinished events of a parent's life on the development of a child. "What begins as a feeling in the mother becomes a reality in the child," writes Murray Bowen, an expert in the field of families. The demands that stem from a parent's unconscious interests are never spoken directly but are woven in at a subliminal level to be picked up by the child. The youngster, by a process of trial and error, always observant, with a keen ear, discovers how to behave in accordance with what the parent needs.

A man, speaking of his childhood relationship with his mother, said to me: "I could tell a mile away what was expected of me." At what age had he perfected his decoding ability? "As far back as I can remember," he said. "You see, she was not young when I was born, and if I made her angry she might have had a heart attack." His mother lived until she was over eighty. Her death didn't release him from his habit of checking out, figuring out, and interpreting what someone wants of him, even though it doesn't work as well with his women friends as it did with his mother. He goes through his life accommodating to his mother's needs, long after she is dead.

It is commonly accepted that our unconscious is the repository for our most threatening memories, feelings, and tendencies, especially those parts of ourselves that we consider negative—what Jung called our "shadow." Jung believed that what is unconscious does not simply stay benign and buried. We may banish our unassimilated experiences, but they still wield power over us. They victimize us and those around us. An internal battle rages: the urge to expose and finish up the incomplete experiences versus continuing to deny them and block them out.

To finish up with our negative and threatening shadow we must bring into the light what we have accumulated in our emotional storage bin. Who wants to do such a thing? Like a bogeyman lurking in the closet, it seems much too frightening to look at. The longer we don't look, the more powerful it grows, the more fearful we get, the more guarded, the more careful to avoid any contact with it.

This collection of discards plays an important role in how we live our lives with our children. Jung wrote, "Everything unconscious is projected." Whatever aspects of our being we refuse to admit as components or features of ourselves, we will surely conjure up in those around us. The attitudes, feelings, and characteristics that we exclude as parts of ourselves, we project onto others, just as an image is projected onto a screen.

As reluctant as we are to meet the shadow within and do battle, we are eager to meet our projected material and defeat it outside of ourselves. That seems much safer. A woman related this bit of her history to me:

> "My father always wanted me to be more orderly. He gave me that book by Thomas Mann to read, *Disorder and Early Suffering*, but I never read it. I often have dreams about having to make order."
>
> Later she said with much concern, "My son is in a serious state of disorder."

Children present themselves as perfect screens upon which parents can project unconscious aspects of themselves. Children are conveniently available. Defenseless and dependent, they are captive. They have neither the words nor the concepts to speak up, to voice objections. Even if they could say what is going on, a flat denial from the parent would be enough to eliminate any further discussion. Besides, a child has no other relationships to compare with. Being a screen for the projections of others becomes the norm, often for life.

Here is the same theme—a mother externally fighting her own inadequacies—with a different issue, taken from *The Doctor's Wife* by Brian Moore:

> "My mother died just last spring."
> "I suppose you still miss her?"

"I don't know. We fought a lot. She once called me a born liar. I don't think I ever forgave her for that."

He laughed. "Why did she say it?"

"Oh, when I was small I was always making up stories about myself. That I was an explorer's daughter, or related to some famous person. Anything but the truth—that I was Sheila Deane of 18 Chichester Terrace, Belfast, a very ordinary little girl."

"And for that she called you a born liar?"

"Yes, I suppose she wasn't too bad, really. Poor Kitty. Funny, when I think of her now, it's always with a cigarette in her mouth, the cigarette bobbing up and down as she talks. She was a great storyteller and people loved to hear her yarns."

In the story "The Dance," Isaac Bashevis Singer presents a good example of projection. He describes a woman who, unaware of her aggression, projected it onto her husband, and later onto her son. The story tells of a beautiful, talented, young woman married to an artist who began to beat her immediately after the wedding. They lived together for two years, had a son, and were divorced, after which she lived alone with their son. For years she talked about her husband's brutality toward her. She herself was never brutal. To hit someone or be directly hostile was something she would never do. *She* played the role of the loving and giving martyr; *they* were brutal. She said in regard to her husband, "I loved him too much. This was my misfortune. The more loving I was, the more vicious he became." Then, about her son, "He is the same. He strikes me,

25

just the same as his father did. . . . Once my darling son blackened my eye." Her husband could, and did, divorce her; her son could not.

What happens to the child who is used as a projection screen? Like a plant that always has the same side to the sun, growth is uneven. One side is underdeveloped and sparse. The other side is overdeveloped; there's too much of it. A warp begins in the child that fulfills for the parent(s) some emotional need. Psychiatrist Murray Bowen quotes a teenage boy, "It's hard to hold my mother's hand and play baseball at the same time." He had to stay helpless for his mother. His babyhood was well-nourished; his growth toward independence never saw the light.

In the Singer story the son's brutality, induced by his mother, was well developed. In a sense he was being brutal *for* his mother. But his capacity to be loving and tender was not developed. His mother had the monopoly on that. Of course, she wasn't truly loving; she was merely a caricature of a loving mother. So at the same time that she needed the child to project onto, to use as a receptive screen, she took something away from him. In this case the mother projected (gave away) her capacity to be brutal and took away her son's capacity to be loving. It was through a fierce need, sometimes experienced as love, that the mother and son became irretrievably entangled and lived out their lives together doing their dance.

Having projected onto someone else what they don't want, people then take up battle against the projection. Parents, having lost, or fearing to lose, the struggle against some negative force that threatens from their shadow, will use their child unknowingly as adversary, perhaps hoping to win the war this time around.

The mother of the so-called retarded boy seemed overly eager to get rid of the child, to send him away to a home for mentally handicapped children. When their therapist insisted on seeing the parents and the boy, saying she would not recommend a facility until she had sized up the situation for herself, the father seemed relieved that there might be other options for the child. The mother, on the other hand, had abandoned all hope and was eager to make the decision where to send the boy. It was as if she had to banish the boy as she had banished the guilt and fear connected to her brother.

The following restaurant scene is an illustration of a father fighting out with his daughter his internal battle to achieve "perfection." Mother, father, daughter, and guest are at the table, looking at menus. Father asks everyone, "What do you want for your first course?" Mother and daughter both want spaghetti. Father says to daughter, "No spaghetti for you; it's too fattening. You have the juice or the melon. Now, what will you have for your main dish?" Everyone at the table answers except the daughter. "Well, what do you want?" demands the father. "I don't know," spoken softly. "What do you mean you don't know what you want? You have to learn to make up your mind!"

This domineering father is always certain about what he wants. He is certain about how he should be and how other people, especially his wife and daughter, should be. He has no feelings of ambiguity or weakness. He exercises every day and gets on the scale regularly. Could he ever be undecided? Wishy-washy? Did he ever have the secret wish to be sloppy or irresponsible? Not he! But he invents in his daughter these unacceptable desires. Of course she is young and human; perfection has escaped her. At twelve she has gotten a bit chubby.

The scene in the restaurant demonstrates what the battle looks like. The father transfers his internal struggle against his own imperfection to an external struggle against what he considers his daughter's imperfection. The same harshness he brings to bear internally against himself, he brings to bear on her.

Consider a woman who has a conflict about her sexuality. Since she was a young girl she has known that "nice girls don't feel sexy." She has spent years denying any sexual desires or enjoyment. She puts up with her husband and his "animal desires." This woman has a daughter who was the sexiest little three-year-old on the block. At the age of nine the little/big girl is dressed in low-neck dresses; at fourteen she gets pregnant. Her mother is shocked and will have nothing to do with her. Vehemently she accuses her with all of the epithets: whore, slut, loose woman, et cetera. These are the very same words her own mother had used on her. The bogeyman in this woman's closet is her sexuality. She won't let it out of the closet any more than her mother did. To accept her sexuality and become a full woman is apparently too threatening. Yet unwittingly she projects her sexuality onto her daughter, and when it appears before her she must fight it.

Both the mother in this example above and the father in the restaurant had eliminated what they considered weakness or evil in themselves through denial. Fragmented, they projected out what they struggled to conquer. They were still at war, only now they fought with the projected characteristic in the child.

Sometimes when parents are losing the struggle to be good and upright, to reach unrealistic ideals, they also use their children as adversaries, perhaps hoping for another chance to win. Children can't always fight back, as the following case taken from the report "Persons in Need of Supervision," by Lis Harrison, in the August 14, 1978, *New Yorker*, makes tragically clear.

Being afraid that her daughter would be like her—a loose woman—and make the same mistakes she had, a mother filed petitions and went through a series of court hearings resulting in her daughter's being put in a facility with children who had committed murder, theft, and arson. The report on the daughter, Rosa, was that she was "an extraordinarily sweet and alert girl with a cautious, gentle, manner," and all of twelve years old! The mother hardly knew the child since Rosa was in foster care for seven years after she was born and then lived with her grandmother. The mother, meanwhile, "brought many strange men into her apartment at night." Imagining her daughter to be a carrier of her own weakness, she succeeded in having Rosa spend the next six years in shelters and various state institutions, including a psychiatric ward.

This account is notable for several reasons. First, it points out the damage that is done when a parent conjures up in the child, and then declares war on, his or her own shadow. Second, it reminds us of the extremes that a parent will go to in order to annihilate that aspect of his or her personality which is projected onto the child. Third, it brings to our attention how absolutely irrelevant the reality of the child is to the parent who sees only his or her projection. In this case the mother almost never saw Rosa, yet she accused her of all sorts of wrongdoing. She was fighting in her daughter what she couldn't control in herself. The final point to mention in this account is how the mother used the courts and the legal system against her powerless daughter. Parents may bring in the "big guns"—be they God, Santa Claus, or the law—when they need to control or defeat a part of themselves they have projected onto a child.

A father who needed to be the strong, capable caretaker interfered with his daughter's growth toward independence. The woman who told me this story was well into her forties. Her father had been her rescuer ever since she could remember. There was no predicament she would get into that he could not, with his money or power, get her out of. From childhood to adulthood she kept him busy and feeling needed as she got into one scrape after another, each more serious than the last. It all culminated in her severe alcoholism and a series of attempts at suicide. One day her father came to her with tears in his eyes and said quietly, "I can't afford to keep you any longer." That was the turning point in her life. She described that time as a moment of profound meeting between the two of them, and the beginning of the development of her own strength and capabilities. Only when the father admitted *his* incapability could the daughter admit her capability.

Imagine if a parent said to a child, "I have this crippled leg; I don't want it. You take it, and let me use yours. If you don't let me use yours, I won't love you. I might even die." The child offers a nice healthy leg, which the parent then depends on. But the new leg doesn't really fit the parent, and of course it never grows. So both parent and child hobble along together. Neither becomes whole.

Psychologically, parents do the identical thing. They project a part of themselves that they don't want onto the child; let's say, laziness, sexuality, obstinacy, or brutality. Then they help themselves to a part of the child in an attempt to become whole. But this part that they take never fits, never develops, never is assimilated into the system. It never works as hoped.

Whatever way a parent needs a child emotionally will in some way distort the growth of the child. A boy came to a therapist's office accompanied by his mother, father, and sister. He was nine, big for his age, and was considered a problem because he got into fights and swore a lot. His father said, "He can't control himself." During the interview the father talked about himself as a young child. He was always big for his age, got into fights, and even as an adult he couldn't control his swearing. In fact, he tended to "lose control of himself," and had recently pulled a telephone out of the wall at work.

The father had his accessory, his accomplice in his fight with society. He had actually groomed his son to be his twin. Although he *said* that he wanted his son to shape up, at every opportunity he related with apparent delight how much the son was just like he was. With a big grin, he told how the son "got back at the neighbors" with whom the parents had a running battle. The son was roped in to fight for his parents with the outside world. The boy's natural tendency to develop appropriate behavior for his age took a backseat to his father's needs.

A woman related this story of how she lived out a romance for her mother:

> I married my mother's dream man. He was only three years younger than she and I really think she was in love with him the whole time I was married to him. I wondered sometimes whether they were having an affair. For me it was the most painful period of my life. When we got divorced my mother was heartbroken. She has never forgiven me.

This woman's mother attempted to live out through her daughter what she never had had for herself. It didn't work for either of them. The daughter needed to make her own decisions about whom she loved, to learn from trial and error what *she* wanted. Her mother needed to find her own man, make her own commitment, and create her own romance.‘

Parents are people, and like all others they attempt to get what they need from the world around them, including the people nearest to them. Their emotional exploitation of their children may be unintentional but it is no less evil and damaging for that. The child is shaped as the parent needs. A son's or daughter's distorted growth is the puzzle piece that is supposed to complete the parent's emotional picture. Both parent and child end up incomplete.

Autonomy and independence, necessities if one is to develop to maturity and move on from being a child to becoming an adult, are hard to come by when parent and child share some piece of emotional anatomy. Like Siamese twins they are joined.

Children may have physical symptoms, nightmares, or problems with friends and school as a result of being used for parents' needs. They don't come out unscathed. They may feel frustrated, fearful, perhaps resentful. Yet they are unequipped to confront a parent directly. The parent may be the source of problems for the child, but more important, the parent is the source of contact, of nourishment, of survival. A child will not jeopardize the relationship that exists, no matter how tenuous it may be.

This is true for older children as well. A man told of being his father's sexual partner from the time he was twelve years old all through his teen years. He knew it wasn't right or good, yet he felt trapped. Whom could he go to? Not his mother. He had to protect her, as he protected his father. Not to anyone outside the family. His father had high status in the community. Who would believe him, anyway? Whenever the father felt his son pulling away, he would threaten to find another boy to take his place. This got the son every time. He extricated himself, finally, at the age of twenty-one.

The emotional attachments that develop are not unilateral but, rather, parallel. The more a parent needs the child emotionally, the more the child becomes emotionally dependent. The potentials of both are underdeveloped, not through evil intent on the part of the parent or the child, but rather through ignorance and fear and looking out for one's interests in what seems the safest way. As they hobble along together it becomes impossible to separate one's interests from the other's. The fear of becoming free of bonds comes to hold equal terror for parent and child.

Meryle Secrest, in her biography of artist Romaine

Brooks, quotes her at eighty-five: "My mother comes between me and life." Her mother had been dead for years, but that didn't matter. She still provided a feeble support, a useful excuse for this woman who imagined she could not make her own decisions.

A young child's interests are closely tied to a parent's interests; therefore it's not hard for a frightened and needy mother or father to hook into a frightened and needy child. A single parent may draw a child into an especially close bond, sometimes resembling a surrogate partner. To quote James Agee in *Let Us Now Praise Famous Men*, "In her dry agony of despair a mother may fasten her talons and her vampire mouth upon the soul of her struggling son and drain him empty, light as a locust shell."

An adult woman told me, as she complained about having to call her father every week, "I hate to take care of him, but I have to. I always have." "He has no wife?" I asked. "Oh yes, but she doesn't take care of him." "He doesn't call you?" "Oh, no. The same with his mother. He has to take care of her and call her every week." Her father was fifty-five years old, but age is irrelevant. She had been his emotional rock since she could remember and she knew no way to exit from that emotional involvement.

3 | Our Safety: How Our Children Add to It and Take It Away

When our daughter was sixteen, I remember her saying to me, "You ask me how I feel and when I tell you, you get mad at me." Now, fourteen years later, I realize how this sensitive, intense girl threatened my safety with her feelings. What parents need in relation to their children is closely allied to what parents need to feel safe. By the time we are adults and parents, we have secured ourselves behind a fortress of beliefs, values, and familiar ways of being. Our primary interest is most often in just staying there.

Children hourly come up with unexpected and inconvenient ways to challenge us. They haven't yet learned what's what and who's who, according to our definitions. They ask questions. "Daddy, why did you go back in the bathroom and put a towel around you?" A father told me that his five-year-old daughter asked him that question. Being a conscientious father he wanted to be honest, but he really didn't know why. "A father shouldn't be naked before his daughter," he answered, recalling that somewhere in the Bible it is so written. "Why not?" came the next question. Many parents would begin to feel uncomfortable at this point and put an end to the talk. "It's not customary." "What's customary? Is that the same as a law?" The father of this bright child thought a bit when he was off by himself about how he had answered his daughter and judged himself rather harshly as dishonest. The true answer, he decided, was, "I don't feel comfortable naked in front of you."

We often don't feel comfortable with our children. They throw us off balance. Their questions seem abrasive, frequently critical; their actions, disconcerting. They bring home friends who are the "wrong" sort. They tell us straight out that what we believe doesn't make sense. They grow their hair too long or cut it too short, they criticize our lifestyles, they embrace new religions. Their very existence slashes through the tough membrane of amnesia that separates us from the painful memories of our own infancy and childhood.

We are comfortable when we feel safe, when we know what to expect of people and places. We enjoy knowing that we can cope. We want to feel that we can manage. We don't like situations that threaten us, that make us unsure. We don't like people who make us feel unsafe either. We are uncomfortable for fear they could knock us off balance. We resent them, we blame them, we close off our hearts: "He isn't going to touch me." We close our minds: "There's no way I can understand him. Nor do I want to."

It is natural to want to feel comfortable with ourselves and our surroundings. Much of what we do in our lives assures us the security that we need to be at ease. From the place where we live, to the newspaper we read, to the friends we choose, we arrange as much as we can to preserve the familiar and avoid the unknown. Some people might feel safe in the middle of the Atlantic, alone in a twenty-foot sailboat; others need the solid earth under their feet, a familiar roof over their heads, their family around them.

Our children decimate our feelings of security; they seem, at times, a dangerous element in our lives. For some of us the first sign of the first pregnancy is accompanied by questions of self-doubt: Will I be able to manage? Will I be a good parent? We are unsure, anxious, or threatened. Dr. T. Berry Brazelton, author and pediatrician, likes to meet the parents-to-be of his future charge. He reassures them that, eager as they are for the big day to finally arrive, it is not uncommon to feel unprepared for actually becoming parents. Part of the problem is we don't want to be just any parent. We have high standards for ourselves; we want to do a good job.

This fact in itself can bring its share of anxiety. For some, even before the birth, the child is causing discomfort and apprehension similar to what they have known facing an exam. Will they pass the tests that await them in this new stage of life? These feelings are compounded when people tell themselves they shouldn't feel unsure. How can a baby who isn't yet born be so threatening? It doesn't make sense. True to human fashion, we deny everything so we can feel safe again.

New parents are not the only ones who have misgivings about their ability to do their job well. At many points in a parenting career, what we do with our children is on a collision course with what we think we ought to do. With all the books for parents and the high value put on parenthood these days, many people have lofty and unrealistic standards for themselves: They should always be nice, they should always know what their child needs, they should accept their child as an individual, they should never feel impatient. We struggle to maintain these standards.

Our misgivings propel us away from safety and ease. How unsettling when we know we are good, decent, and loving parents and at the same time we are feeling or acting in a way that doesn't fit in with our picture of a good, decent, loving parent. Whether we are secretly wishing we could get away from a crying infant, or silently wondering how much longer before the teenager will go and leave us in peace, our irritation with the child is compounded with displeasure in ourselves: I am not as I always thought I was; I am not as I think I should be.

The reality of having the child in our arms and finding we do manage after all scatters some of the early uncertainty about becoming a parent. Resentments melt in the face-to-face interaction: How little! how perfect! how adorable! On the other hand, new threats and resentments emerge, and interfere with our comfort and safety. One mother told me that her new baby's eyes were "just like her father's—so sad." Each time she looked at those sad eyes she saw disapproval and accusation. Another mother tells of feeling overwhelmed by her child's helplessness. What if she forgot to hold up his head? Yet another mother voiced the fear of many when she disclosed that she was in terror of dropping her daughter.

Much of our security in day-by-day living rests in knowing what the world is all about and how we fit into it. Without that knowledge, we would experience chaos. We get a touch of that sensation when we are in a new country. We don't know the language. The surroundings are unfamiliar. In such a situation we stave off confusion and uneasiness by getting our bearings. We look at a map; we get the lay of the land. For the most part, we get our bearings by fitting in what we and others do to what we know about ourselves, people in general, and the world. We need to be able to explain and make sense of ourselves and others according to what we have learned, our time-tested beliefs, what we accept as true. When people and events fit into "how things should be," we have no cause to worry.

We are constantly sizing up situations and making judgments, seeing that everything fits into some category that we are familiar with. "That man's crazy." "That woman is dressed funny, but she looks nice." "That child acts strange." From our judgments we decide what to do. "He's crazy. I'm not going to pay any attention to him." "She looks nice. Maybe I could ask her where this bus goes." "The child must be lost. I'll see if I can help him." In each of those cases we fit what we see with our knowledge of what is normal, right, and sane.

What we know about for certain is who we are, what we are like, what we do and don't do. "I'm the kind of person who always . . ." "If I were in that situation I would . . ." "She suggested doing such and such, but being who I am, of course I said no." Not to recognize ourselves is a most upsetting, even frightening experience. The ground turns slippery under us. "I can't believe I did that. I don't know what came over me. I wasn't myself." "What I did doesn't make sense to me. I'm worried about myself." "I'm not who I thought I was."

We come to know who we are largely by how our parents defined us, but those definitions often had more to do with our parents than with us. One parent defines negatively as "obstinate" the very same behavior that another parent defines positively as "having a mind of one's own." From our earliest days we knew from their facial expressions, voices, and touch what was good about us and what was bad. Aggression, meanness, sexuality, selfishness—such qualities and the actions they inspired were not acceptable. So many of us became very good at hiding behind screens of smiles, or indifference, or polite ways that were "pleasanter to live with." We put those qualities that were frowned upon out of our lives, out of our awareness; they ceased to be part of us, except in special places and situations where they were considered suitable.

Then along come our children to poke holes in our screens. They force us to meet the creatures inside ourselves. One father, a gentle, quiet minister, confessed, "I never knew I could be so angry as I get with my son. I don't recognize myself." Not only do we resent people who bring out the worst in us, we resent those who see us at our worst, who know what we don't even want to know about ourselves.

Our view of ourselves, our philosophy, our values are not just passing fancies. They are the ground on which we stand. Without that solid footing we might fall into chaos. Like self-hypnosis, we lull ourselves into comfort with our truisms: "Good always wins out in the end." "Children should respect their elders." "Girls should be interested in how they look." In "All in the Family," Archie Bunker was the prototypical father who was threatened by anything different from his "little girl." She was to be happy, smiling, respectful, and a good helper to her mother in the kitchen.

We have confidence in our everyday brand of knowledge; it works for us in explaining ourselves and our actions, our experiences, and other people. We depend on our old beliefs; we cherish them and the certainty they impart to us. We don't hesitate to pull a convenient platitude out of a pocket to reinforce or defend what we have come to accept as the way things are, or the way people are: "Give an inch and they'll take a mile," for example. We use any means we have to avoid the turmoil that seems sure to descend on us if our old conceptions are threatened.

Behavior that doesn't look right is upsetting, especially when it is our own or our children's. Youngsters, simply because they are by nature lively, curious, and innocent, can make us uncomfortable with how they are and what they do. For one thing, they are spontaneous. Not yet bound by the social dictates of being polite, they do what they have to do wherever they may be. They make noises, they say what comes into their heads to say. Not aware of others' feelings they point and stare. Not looking where they go they step on toes.

They express themselves. That in itself probably threatens more parents than anything else. Fearful as we are of losing control, we have generally flattened out our own self-expression beyond recognition. We believe that being out of control is bad and crazy; therefore our children should be in control of themselves, as we are. We don't want crazy kids. For an extremely constrained parent a child squirming with delight, making strange, loud, squealing noises, waving arms and kicking little legs can be very frightening. Might not such a sensualist get into a lot of trouble later on? So the parent tries to nip such behavior in the bud.

This is one woman's story in a nutshell: "When I was twenty-one I read everything Freud had written. I went to my mother and said, 'You sure made a mouse out of me.'" "But dear," answered her mother, "you were always like that." Twenty years later, in a more honest moment, her mother told her, "You sure were a spunky baby when you were around eighteen months, but we spanked that out of you." This woman remembers herself as a little girl walking around the house saying, "I'm seven and I'm perfect."

Those parents who have known much fear and pain in their own lives will sometimes become overcontrolling in their efforts to protect not so much their children, but rather themselves from having to experience more fear, directly or indirectly. A man told me of his mother, "She lived her whole life in terror. She was afraid of everything—the dark, people she didn't know, storms. You name it, she was afraid of it." She controlled the lives of her husband and children as much as she could, as long as she could, so that they wouldn't add to her fear. They had to be home before dark, they learned not to ask about death or about anyone who had died, they could not leave her in the house alone.

Children's self-expression, before it is repressed, corrupted, or distorted by overcontrolling parents, is free and exuberant, a natural part of being alive and responding to the world. They try out new sounds, actions, and words, and play at getting reactions from grown-ups, but to parents their freedom and exuberance may come across like the enemy to battle and defeat with every weapon available. What we can't deal with in ourselves we feel even less safe with in our children.

One couple who had a severely disturbed sixteen-year-old told how their daughter was their "little doll" until she was almost five. Then she said, "Goddamn you" to her father. To judge how serious a threat this was, consider the retaliation. The father washed out her mouth with Tabasco sauce, hot mustard, and soap. The mother, in relating the incident many years later, said the little girl went around the house holding a wet cloth to her tongue to ease the burning, all the time saying, "Goddamn you, Goddamn you." This was the beginning (as they tell it; the real beginning was years before that) of a long history of severe problems with the "little doll." The parents were angry but controlled people. They themselves said "bad words" occasionally. But when they heard "Goddamn you" from their daughter, their buttons were pushed. That behavior was unacceptable. They did not allow themselves to act out and they would not allow their daughter that freedom either. But using all of their ammunition did not do the trick. Quite the contrary. She never did learn to restrain herself. Instead she became an out-of-control, compulsive swearer. The parents didn't even have the illusion of control. They couldn't take her out in public. Especially in public she would let loose with the most offensive language.

Another example is a mother who at the age of twenty-five still sucked her thumb. A friend of hers reported that she was present when this woman gave birth to her first child, a son. About five hours after the birth the mother was holding him when the clever little tyke found his thumb and started sucking. The mother immediately took it out of his mouth, saying, "Don't suck your thumb. We won't have any of that."

A young mother was in court for murdering her child. She had followed her soldier husband a long way from home. She was isolated, lonely, and bored with only an infant for company. Trying to explain her brutal behavior toward the child, she told the judge, "I couldn't stand it when she started to scream. It drove me crazy." The young woman had tried to hold herself together in her new surroundings. She herself couldn't risk "letting down" and crying for fear of losing the semblance of control she maintained. In the words of sociologist T. J. Scheff, in his book *Catharsis in Healing, Ritual, and Drama*, "The more repressed emotion one has accumulated, the less one can tolerate discharge in others, since it disturbs one's own equilibrium." She repressed her own crying and she couldn't handle her infant's crying. Seeing and hearing her child cry was too threatening; she had to stop it. The tragedy was she lost her equilibrium completely.

It seems clear that the most extreme physical and emotional abuse on the part of parents is provoked by youngsters' upsetting one's feeling of safety. Sometimes it is what the child is actually doing, like soiling, crying, or even laughing, that is intolerable; in other instances, what the parent is afraid the child might do, like become a prostitute or in some way a misfit, pushes the parent over the edge.

Life is so much more serene when we can be sure our children agree with and reinforce our view of the world. How easy when we are all of like mind. Our kids learn early if a differing point of view upsets us. Periodically they arrive from school with, "My teacher said . . ." and they watch for the reaction. Or, "My friend's mother said that anyone who votes for X is a communist." In some families parents assume that the children will agree with the "family outlook." The message is, If you don't agree with us, you are not one of us. On the family car is a sticker: OUR FAMILY SUPPORTS X FOR PRESIDENT.

One of the sharpest blows to parental complacency comes when children reject the values, ideas, and beliefs that we hold dear. That makes us anxious with uncertainty. When dissonant ideas come our way we are threatened, and when these ideas are presented by our own children at our dining room table, we are doubly threatened. Here is our flesh and blood embracing disturbing, even subversive notions. This seems like an act of betrayal; they are anti-us. Here we have given them life, straightened their teeth, fed them all these years—is it so much to ask that they should conform?

If parents don't push their philosophy, they fear the next generation might espouse another. What if they do something "crazy" like go off to art school when we've groomed them for medical school, or take up some social cause that we can't understand, or, heaven forbid, follow a strange guru to India? To ward off any such threat, parents may try to isolate their children from people, books, magazines, and films that present a different outlook on society, politics, or religion. Censorship, however, rarely achieves its purpose. Children seem compelled to direct their boundless energy and passions in all new areas. Parental bans often backfire. If a child wants to spite his or her parents, what better way than to seek out and embrace the enemy, to thumb the nose at the old friends, the favored political party, or at the church?

Our safety seems a precarious commodity, ready to vanish unexpectedly with any manner of threat from our children. The more we need it, the more precarious it is. Threats come in many guises. This letter, written to Ann Landers, is one example:

> Last night I did something that really frightened me. I was helping our son with his homework and he refused to try to solve the math problem—just kept saying, "I can't get it." I became so infuriated I started to slap his face as hard as I could and I couldn't stop. Today the little guy was black-and-blue-marked on his cheeks. I was so ashamed I didn't let him go to school.

What threatens the safety of one parent may not touch another. It depends on where our own demons lie: what the emotional issues are in our lives, in what areas we are still dangling or dissatisfied from our own childhood, what secret fears and feelings we are harboring. For one parent a son who isn't interested in the family fortune may be intolerable. For another, it is the child who laughs when the parent gets angry. Some parents are particularly upset by a child who simply looks distressed.

That we are concerned about safety in this life is something understandable. We have experienced our own methods of self-protection and are aware that others protect themselves from the unusual, the novel, the threatening. To some degree we are aware when the limits of what feels safe begin to push in on us and we know how we plan our lives to keep chaos at bay. According to a prominent social theorist, Ernest Becker, most of us are unconscious of another critical area of vulnerability: safety and comfort when this life is over. That is, we want some assurance that we will triumph over death, that we will, in some form, be immortal. Whether we are members of a formal religion or not, whether we are conscious or not of hoping to sit at the right hand of God in the next life, many aspects of our lives are influenced by this motivation, although it is generally unacknowledged.

Holding the "right" values and beliefs is one way to please the powers that be. Becker lists others: belonging to the "right" church, being on the "right" side, marrying the "right" partner, giving money to the "right" causes, and having children who do the "right" things and go to the "right" schools. Many people live their whole lives convincing themselves that they are doing the right things and are indeed worthy. In that way they rest secure that they will continue on after death.

When our children challenge our way of life, it is a serious matter, more serious by far than simply, What will the neighbors think? Their lives are part of our lives; their fate, our fate. When they reject our values, our ideas, they say, in effect, I have another way that is right. But how can they be right when we, as parents, believe *we* know what is right? We have lived our lives according to a set of rules based on beliefs. Perhaps we have accepted the teachings of a church. Now, when confronted by our children, how can we dare think we might be wrong? To be wrong means that our entire life has no meaning. To be wrong is to lose out on immortality. Or our children are wrong, in which case they are forfeiting their rights to heaven through their stupidity and pigheadedness.

This may seem like an exaggeration until we consider the tragic scenes that are played out in families when children make choices in opposition to their parents' most deeply held beliefs. Issues take on a life-and-death importance. Consider the vehemence with which parents have turned their children out of their homes for choosing a different creed. In some religions it is customary for parents to grieve for a son who marries out of his religion as if the son were dead. He is dead for them.

This is serious business; the stakes are high for parents who depend on the help of their children to work out their salvation. What a crashing disappointment, and how unforgivable, when a child jeopardizes their chances. As parents have felt and said in moments of extreme disappointment, "Now my whole life is meaningless."

Yes, many of our efforts for safety in relation to our children miscarry. Yet in many ways it is through our children that we do acquire safety and feelings of well-being.

Children provide us with people in our lives. This we want. We need to be connected to others. Belonging is basic for achieving some degree of safety in life. Historically people have formed groups: families, tribes, and nations. From our earliest days we ourselves have been part of some group. Without a group to identify with we are alone, drifters, exiles. Our children are a bridge connecting us with others: with family members, with neighbors, with new friends.

Through our children we come up to the status of our parents. We are part of the group of parents at church, school, scouts, music lessons, sports competitions, and all the rest. Through our children we belong.

Children fill out a family for us. A couple does not seem a family the way a couple with children is a family. All the fantasies we have had of having our own family can now be reality because we are parents. We are a link to the past and a part of the future.

Needing to be needed—how children give that satisfaction! They do need us, no question, and we derive satisfaction in many different arenas. Our days have substance, our lives have meaning, life and work seem more worthwhile. We are grounded in the knowledge that we are of supreme importance to someone—our child. This is permanent. For the rest of our lives, we will be parents.

Love, too, we need. Some of us are blessed and have a partner who loves us; we may still have parents or grandparents who show care and concern out of their love for us. Yet the love of children is a different kind of love. They care about us and express their love in the way that children do, not lovers or parents. They love us partly for selfish reasons, since their security rests on our security. Yet their actions are not always motivated by selfishness, as when a youngster saves every cent of his allowance to buy a birthday present for Mother. A headline in the newspaper describes an extreme example: BOY, 13, HANGS SELF TO EASE MOTHER'S BURDEN.

Through our children life grants us a second chance for the success and honors that may have escaped us. "My son the doctor." "Our daughter the actress." "My son the philanthropist." The glory rubs off on us. We find ourselves accorded a new respect. We are reassured that we are good people and have done a good job. We possess a new self-esteem. Our stock goes up, in this world and for the next.

We use our interaction with our children to fill our emotional voids. These voids are generally more hidden from us than from them. As mentioned in the previous chapter, we have the teenager Bowen described, who said so eloquently that he could not hold his mother's hand and play baseball at the same time. His mother didn't have to demand that he hold her hand. Most likely she never considered that she needed her son this much, yet her behavior was a constant indication to him that she wanted him to hold her hand, not literally but symbolically. As children will when they experience their parent as needy, he did his best to fill the bill— symbolically. Apparently the mother in this case felt more secure with a disturbed, dependent son than with a normal boy who would become independent and leave her.

An unwed mother of a year-old son told a friend on several occasions, "I'm so happy to have this love object in my life." What happens to a child who is so important to his mother as an object of love? He is there to make up for a deficiency in her life. Rather than being free to grow fully, he is destined to grow in the shape and direction that his mother needs in her attempt to become whole. As we will see in subsequent chapters, this stunts the growth of both. Similarly a son whose mother needed him to be her companion; he didn't have much of a childhood but he learned to be an excellent escort. His manners were impeccable.

Secure emotional footing depends in large part on the ground remaining solid beneath us. We depend on those close to us, especially our children, to shore up potentially shaky places. What gives us security doesn't always make sense, is not necessarily rational. Most often what we need in order to avoid cave-ins is to hold onto our illusions and stay as we know we are. To stay on solid ground we need to repeat the familiar interactions that bring familiar feelings. If our familiar emotional state is made up of questioning our worth, feeling victimized or guilty, then we are likely to induce that behavior from our children which will keep us in our familiar state.

In Singer's story "The Dance," mentioned earlier, the woman needed a partner to abuse her, to make her a martyr. Her husband, who played that role in her life for two years, once said after a glass of vodka, "The fact that I did not kill her proves that I am a saint." She later induced in her son the same brutal behavior. She complained about him as she did her husband, but she apparently thrived in her customary role. As long as her son lived she was guaranteed that her appetite for abuse would be satisfied. She would be victimized for being "too loving."

If we need to feel "king of the mountain," our children will be lesser beings at the foot of our mountain. If we need to compete, we ourselves will have a competitor. If we need to be a child, we will reverse the roles and make our child into our parent. If we need to be needed, we will infantilize a child who will need us forever.

It is through such covert needs that parents interfere with their children's growth. A child becomes a narcissistic extension of the parent, an emotional straightman whose main function is to put into the parent's life what the parent needs to feel safe or whole.

Parents frequently find it convenient to put their children in the third corner of a triangle. It often happens that couples exploit a child to help submerge their marital problems. This is done in various ways. Whereas it might seem extremely risky to face up to marital issues, a couple might argue for years about a child, involve themselves in every detail of their son's or daughter's life, thus distracting themselves from a disagreeable or boring marriage. In this way they keep their marriage intact and avoid coming to grips with their relationship problems. A child who is used this way is bound to suffer. The parents encroach on each facet of the child's life—each decision about school, friends, sports, or job becomes the cement of the parents' marriage.

Children are extremely sensitive to the interaction between their parents and are alert to what their parents need from them. Frequently they understand that their job is to hold the family together. Parents' breaking up is most threatening to youngsters. They will go through all kinds of contortions to prohibit that event. In extreme cases they will sacrifice their health and their sanity. One son, even after his parents were divorced, kept up his attempts to reunite them. His way was to get into trouble. When he was picked up by the police, both parents would be called in and they would all sit down together and talk. One day the boy's comment was, "Isn't it good to see them sit down and talk together?"

A family therapist colleague of mine tells the story of a family of three who came to him for counseling. The son is described as a "troubled boy." He has seizures, gets up at night and goes to the parents' room, and is generally unmanageable. The boy completely dominated the therapy sessions to the point that it was altogether impossible for the parents to have a conversation. The child was so intent on interrupting them that finally the therapist positioned himself between the boy and his parents, pushing the boy's chair way into one corner. Then he asked the parents to talk together. From the corner came the boy's voice: "My tooth, my tooth. It's coming out! Look!" And indeed, there in the bloody mouth the tooth hung on by a thread and all attention went back to the boy.

In some marriages what one partner wants is help in staying away from the other partner. What better way than to get the help of a child? As often happens in triangles, one of the three people gets pushed out of the action. Father and daughter carry on a flirtation that leaves Mother out. Sometimes Father and son gang up against Mother, the "men" sticking together, as in this cartoon: A father is shown leaving the house to go to work. He says to his small son in the doorway, "You be the man of the house while Daddy is away, Rodney. Don't let Mommy push you around." Or perhaps it's Mother and daughter against Father. Each time Father criticizes daughter he finds himself in an argument with

Mother. A parent sometimes enlists the help of a child to fight against the other parent: "We're not talking to Daddy tonight." This truly tears a child apart; loyalty to one parent automatically means disloyalty to the other.

In various respects parents need children to do their dirty work, and children bow to the covert demand. They assume their function, really having little choice in the matter. They are dependent. They do what they perceive they must do for their own good and safety. It is important to remember that parents' needs are not talked about explicitly. Children are not apprised of what they have to do for the parents. Plain speaking is not necessary; their intuition is uncanny.

Youngsters are very much in touch with ways of knowing what is going on with parents. They are sensitive to nonverbal cues of voice, body tension, and facial expressions. A couple would never say to a child, "We are having marital problems and we need you to come in our bed every night so that Daddy goes to sleep in the other room." Or, as in the family with the boy with the loose tooth, the parents never told him that they feared it would be dangerous should they talk together without interruption. They didn't need to say, "If we really start to deal with the issues, we might get divorced." Children find a way to answer the unspoken, unspecified need of the parents.

Children used thus in the parents' relationship will most likely develop problems: physical symptoms, psychological symptoms, school problems, delinquency, alcohol and drug problems. The solution that the child devises is acceptable for a while. Otherwise it wouldn't get a toehold. After some time and usually some intensification, it becomes unacceptable. In fact, what was the solution becomes the problem to be solved. The child takes on such unproductive behavior only when the parents, through some need, condone it. Surely two adults can keep a six-year-old boy from constantly interrupting them. And parents can carry a child back to his or her own bedroom. Many parents have been approached by a frightened child, "Can I come in your bed? I'm scared." When they don't need the child to separate them, they will soon get the child out of the marriage bed.

Our beliefs, values, and familiar ways of being are not the secure fortress we may have assumed. The fortress, it seems, has a dungeon that is inhabited by the spooks and demons of our unconscious. And how powerful they are. The more threatening they are to our sense of well-being, the more certain we are to involve our children in our own quest for safety.

4 | Growth Through Relationship

Lena Horne is quoted in an interview: "My mother was either cold as ice or she couldn't do without me. I couldn't stand her. I wanted very much for her to love me. But to the day she died she never told me." In this short quotation, we hear the confusion and frustration of all children who are dependent on and in constant contact with a fragmented parent, one who plays push/pull with the child. "I couldn't stand her," and the very next sentence, "I wanted very much for her to love me." Imagine being dependent for love and nurturing on someone who is like ice, someone who is the enemy. That is the reality for countless youngsters. To add to their confusion, sometimes the enemy turns into a loving parent—but not long enough or consistently enough to trust. That could indeed make someone crazy with anxiety.

Life for the new baby, helpless and dependent in

every way, hangs on the care and love of Mom and Dad. Physical necessities and emotional connections are all wrapped up together: food and warmth. They cannot be separated. They are inextricable. Without food, life isn't possible. Without fondling, holding, emotional connections, a baby gives up the will to live.

There is an implicit and mysterious connection between being loved and growing. We hold, stroke, talk, and sing to our babies. All are forms of emotional fodder absolutely essential to them. A nourishing emotional climate is so important that even when children are undernourished nutritionally, if they have the love and support they need, they actually don't suffer the usual effects of malnutrition. So important is the emotional climate that when there is sufficient food but no connection with another person, chances for survival are slim, as borne out by the history of infant deaths in institutions.

In his book *Touching*, Ashley Montagu tells the grisly statistics of infant deaths in nineteenth- and early-twentieth-century foundling homes. Except for those infants who were taken out for short times and placed in foster homes or with relatives, there generally were no survivors. He tells of an American doctor visiting a children's clinic in Germany in the early days of this century. Asking about a fat old woman who was carrying a "very measly" infant around on her hip, the American doctor was told by the clinic director, "Oh, that is old Anna. When we have done everything we can medically for a baby, and it is still not doing well, we turn it over to old Anna, and she is always successful."

Through interaction with other people, especially

through relating to the parents (traditionally the mother), babies not only get what they need for survival, they learn about themselves—who they are and how they fit into their surroundings. This is a most urgent concern. "I must be important. I must be lovable. Otherwise I may not survive."

Babies find out little by little, step by step, about themselves *as others see them* by the ways others respond. They learn to interpret the looks, actions, and touches of those who care for them. Mother purrs, "Oh, you sweet little thing. You are so special," and gives a gentle hug. The quality of touch, the facial expression of the parent, whether the eyes meet, the tone of voice, all are part of the complete picture, the gestalt of the parent/child interaction, the relating, from which the child begins to learn, Who am I and how do I fit in? Am I important? Am I lovable?

At the same time as they take in how others respond to them, they learn *from their own experience* about themselves and their world. Babies experiment. What behavior, which new accomplishment, which new skill makes an impact and gets a response from others? What kind of response is it? They learn when and how it is possible to get what they need, to manipulate those around them for necessities and pleasures.

Youngsters are pragmatists from the start. Direct experience is their education; what happens to them is true. Cry, and someone comes. Smile, a face smiles back. Bite the nipple, the breast is withdrawn. With the constant broadening of their world come new experiences, other truths. When Daddy comes home Mommy's voice changes. Cry at night, be taken into the parents' bed. When Mommy puts on perfume, she leaves and the baby-sitter comes. Patterns emerge and life feels stable and secure. But life is full of contradictions and confusion as well.

Sometimes the stated information from the outside source doesn't agree with the child's perceptions and impressions. "Yes" sounds like "no," and vice versa. When the child's experience contradicts the parents' words or actions, or when parents contradict themselves or each other, there is bound to be confusion. To misbelieve and mistrust the people you have to depend on leaves only insecurity. It's obligatory when survival depends on parents to believe them. But what of the child's experience, his or her "truth"?

To hold two contradictory truths at the same time takes a kind of psychological sleight-of-hand. When children are thrown on the horns of this dilemma they reject themselves rather than rejecting their parents. They "put away" themselves and their personal experience, and buy the truth that is offered, *even when their own experience screams, "It's a lie!"* They accept their parents' reality and come to mistrust, even deny, their own. Dependent and needy, they have no options but to live in the parents' world.

Children come to see themselves as those around them see them and respond to them; thus their identity forms. When parents tell a child in words or by their actions, "This is how you are," to a large degree they create the child so. The day-by-day, repeated patterns of interaction, beginning early and continuing throughout childhood, create the basis for the identity, for how individuals come to experience and see themselves. "You are lovable," conveyed through words, gestures, and actions, fosters an attitude toward the self quite dif-

ferent from "You are nothing." When the parental attitude is predominantly negative, feelings of low self-
esteem and unworthiness begin to take root in the child.

Our world is full of adults who still buy the long-ago
"truth" of their parents: "I'm no good; I'll never amount
to anything; no one could ever love me if they really
knew me," and all that other nonsense. These people
insist that at "another level" they don't believe any of it,
yet the old fears of losing their parents remain to undermine their self-esteem.

The earliest months of a child's life are chock full of
learning and development. Behavior that "works," that
evokes a response from a parent, is repeated. Dr. Brazelton reports in his book *On Becoming a Family* that
babies as young as four months old will act "phony" to
get a familiar response from a parent. He finds that in
his office a child of that age quickly becomes more interested in the surroundings than in a parent who spontaneously tries to keep his or her attention. But as an
experiment he asked the mothers not to interact with
the child when they came into the office, but simply to
sit, unresponsive, in front of the baby for three minutes. Within *twenty seconds* the child "begins very pur-
posefully to elicit the expected responses from her."

> He brightens up, he smiles, he vocalizes with a coo,
> then a whimper. He fakes a broad smile, a loud pro-
> testing whimper. He may cough or sneeze, and we
> have even had babies who made themselves gag. He
> cannot believe that she won't respond, so he runs
> through his repertoire a second and third time try-
> ing to get her involved with him. If this still-faced,
> unresponsive mother persists, he may give up and

turn actively away, curling up into a protective ball or arching away and closing his eyes as if to try to shut her out in sleep—all of this brought on by only three minutes of changed behavior from her. When she finally does begin to respond and to play with him in the usual manner, he redoubles his responses with obvious joy.

The more children discover about themselves and their world, the less dependent and helpless they become. They discover they can have an effect on things and people. Dr. Brazelton tells of Laura, who learned appropriate sounds for both her mother and her father at seven months. "Her mother spent the first day rushing to her side until she realized that Laura was practicing her skill at saying 'mama.'" What did Laura realize? She discovered a way to have influence on those around her. She could not yet go to her mother, but she could get her mother to come to her. That is power.

The close connection between parent and child, the mutual interest and need, fosters important feelings of worthiness and belonging in a child. Also fostered are the stultifying relationships that develop when the parents' needs are paramount. Parents' needs can blind them to the reality of their child. Then there is no relating. Their responses to their child have little or nothing to do with the actual child and much to do with themselves. When a mother beats her four-month-old son for being "obstinate," this action and this label have to do with her, not the child. However, the child can't make this important discrimination. He takes the attitude of his mother as his attitude toward himself. This particular example is from a book by Barbara Strachey called *Remarkable Relations*, about Hannah Pearsall Smith and her descendants. Smith believed that girls are valuable and boys are not. Her daughters grew up to be strong, gifted women; her son had a depressive nature. He was "introverted and reticent in a world of ebullient female extroverts."

Parents have repetitive and insidious ways of denying a child's reality. One way is to attribute false motives to actions. A two-year-old child reaches out to touch the newly arrived sister. "Oh," says Mother, "you love your little sister." Or a mother having trouble nursing her red-faced, screaming infant for the first time thinks, "I hate this child; he's trying to give me a hard time." Or a parent says to the six-year-old who wet the bed, "You did that to make me mad."

Some parents habitually discourage their children's self-trust and self-expression by telling them what to think, feel, fear, want, etc.

Child: "I want that."
Parent: "No, you don't want that."

Of course what the parent means is "I don't want you to want that."

Child: "I'm afraid."
Parent: "Of course you're not afraid. You're the one who begged to come here in the first place."

Child: "I'm hungry."
Parent: "You can't be hungry, we just ate."

Parents who alternate between kindness and cruelty,

between understanding and rejecting, or as Lena Horne described her mother, between desperately needing the child or being cold as ice, keep a child in a constant state of confusion and anxiety. What is more, the child has no one with whom to check out what is going on. That is something that we all need when we don't understand what is happening. An experiment conducted by psychologist S. Schacter in 1959 with normal adults shows that when they have been startled or frightened they seek out others to be with and talk to, attempting to make sense of or understand whatever has startled or frightened them. Children frequently find themselves in the impossible situation of having only their parents to go to in order to allay fears or help make sense of the capricious situation that stems from the parents themselves.

Consistency of experience is a guiding star to reality for the child. What can be counted on? Is each experience an ephemeral moment, unconnected to what came before? Is there any predictable behavior from others? A dependable view of reality is of supreme importance in the ability to make sense of ourselves and our world, and that is a basic need. It is, in the words of Philip Rieff, "how the naked ego is clothed." It is our handle on some security in this chaotic world.

Children look to parents to make some sense out of the world. When parents bring only more confusion, children are suspended in a state of perpetual uncertainty. This condition is brought on, especially, by the "double bind." This term was coined to describe the situation in which a person will end up badly, with little satisfaction, no matter which action or non-action is chosen. Gregory Bateson first described the classic double bind, which he maintained may, in extreme cases, result in schizophrenia.

There are certain ingredients that go into making up the classic double bind. First of all there must be a dependent relationship. A parent/child relationship is surely that, as we have discussed earlier. The parents are the primary source of care and comfort. This dependence on parents influences a child to do whatever is necessary to get approval and good-will from them.

When love is withdrawn, life is endangered. For a baby, rejection is death. For the rest of us, it may feel like it. "Leave me and I'll die" is the greatest manipulation that adults can use on one another or that a parent can use on a child. For a child this threat is experienced as reality.

The second element necessary for a double bind situation is two paradoxical instructions given at the same time. Most often one of the messages is stated explicitly. The other is implicit in the actions, body posture, or tone of voice. An example of this is a mother who tells her son to "grow up and act your age," but through her actions encourages him to remain a helpless infant. Another example is a mother who complains that her five-year-old son is "driving me crazy." He won't eat. Every meal is a struggle between them. Frequently the mother, in desperation, sits for as long as two hours, telling stories, putting spoonfuls of mashed food into the child's mouth. The mother is an extremely thin woman who dislikes eating. She is clearly using her son for her own eat/don't eat conflict. Although she apparently wants her son to eat, the child hears the unspoken message "Don't eat." What is unspoken is generally the louder message to the child. At his grandmother's house he eats fine.

It may seem that a person would have to be crazy to communicate two contradictory instructions to a child. Yet few of us are of a single mind at all times. Most of us spend a good deal of our lives in a state of ambiguity. Since uncertainty brings anxiety, we usually do a little mental magic and fool ourselves into thinking we are pure and straightforward in our actions and attitudes. The mother mentioned in a previous chapter who fosters her daughter's sexuality only to fight it later is giving double messages, as is the father who told his daughter to choose what she wanted in a restaurant and then overrode her choice. In one moment he says, "Make your own decision." In the next moment he implies, "You can't make your own decision." We may laugh at the joke about the Jewish mother who, after giving her son two shirts for his birthday, asks as he appears wearing one of the shirts, "What's the matter? You don't like the other one?" However, it is not funny for the child who is damned if he does and damned if he doesn't, not just one time but as a general rule, caught in the game of trying to please a parent who can't be pleased.

Usually the message that is explicitly stated is the one that shows the parent in a good light, the stance that is generally acceptable. "I want you to be happy. I'm a reasonable person and I do what is best for you. I want you to learn to be independent and have your own friends." At the same time the child experiences just the opposite from the parent's actions. A mother indirectly blames her daughter in several ways for having her own friends. She may look disappointed when the daughter says she is meeting a friend downtown to go shopping. "But I thought we were going together," Mother pouts. Or she shows in her tone of voice that she doesn't approve of this friend. And the boyfriends will never do! The daughter doesn't know what to believe. "You don't want me to have my own friends," she accuses her mother. "Of course I do, dear. When have I ever said you couldn't have friends? Didn't I suggest you invite Marie for the weekend at the cottage?" "Marie! That baby?" Then the subject gets lost in the argument about whether or not Marie is a baby. The daughter is confused.

The first two requirements for the classic double bind—a dependent relationship and two contradictory or paradoxical instructions given at the same time—are followed by a third. There must be no exit, no way to escape the situation for the one who is dependent. The child cannot walk away, cannot simply leave the family. This is always true for young children, and even after the age of eighteen there are still things that make leaving difficult. Financial considerations are generally pressing, but in families with overinvolved parents, the emotional ties themselves are almost impossible to break.

The fourth requirement is the family rule, implicit but clearly understood, that talking about what is going on is not allowed. There is no "meta-communication," that is, no one in the family says, "This is what I see happening here and this is how I feel." When the daughter in the above example accused her mother of not wanting her to have friends, she was making a feeble attempt to meta-communicate. The mother immediately denied the accusation, and retaliated with an example that would bolster her own case, thereby distracting the daughter. That is just one of many ways of discouraging meta-communication, of denying a child's experience, of communicating, "I am not interested in what you hear, see, or feel." Parents use anything from subtle looks, to automatic disagreement, to unsuppressed hostility: "I don't want to hear what you think."

When all the components of a double bind are present in an ongoing situation, the development of the self is severely damaged. There is an unreal quality to the words and actions of the perpetrator of the double bind. For the child it is like living a play that everyone pretends is real. The child is not seen and not heard. Used merely as an actor with a part to play in a parent's drama, the child remains a stranger to the parent and largely a stranger to himself or herself. The message children get from their world is as follows: "You don't matter. You're not important. Your experience is valid only if it agrees with my [the parent's] experience." The typical reactions of a child are withdrawal or acting out, sometimes in a self-destructive way.

The simplest positive response from another validates one's experience, gives one a sense of self, and imparts feelings of personal power, feelings of accomplishment, of being somebody. Even adults when testing their capabilities in a foreign language are elated when a native actually understands and responds. They are encouraged to try more complex exchanges. Each success leads to further adventures, further experiments, increased confidence. To a child, being seen, heard, and responded to is the beginning of feeling worthy, of trusting oneself, of the development of self-esteem: in short, the foundation of satisfactory relationships in the future.

Central to all human life is relationship. When parents respond to a child so that the child feels he has been seen and heard, they validate the child's existence. The child exists in the eyes of another, and with only this encouragement he is ready to get on with living the next moment of life, growing, exploring, moving into new experiences. Without the validation of a response, all the energy goes into attempts to get attention, as we saw in Dr. Brazelton's description of infants and their mothers in his office. With repeated failure at getting a response, children give up trying. This occurred in only three minutes with the infants who were accustomed to responsive mothers!

Relationship is literally a matter of life and death to young children. To be part of what is going on around them is so important that, whatever the cost to their own development, they will pay. When the parent's existence is threatened by the growth of selfhood in the child, the child will hide or distort this growth in order to protect the parent.

There seems to be no end to what children will do for parents, even to the detriment of their own well-being and healthy development. Yet we can't deny that children also gain in some way from the transactions. Eight-month-old Laura, one of the children described by Dr. Brazelton and mentioned earlier, is not an unwilling accomplice as she acts helpless in front of her parents. Her helplessness serves the function of making her parents hover more; their hovering serves to make her more helpless. As long as they straighten her up each time she falls forward and bring toys within her reach, she remains a helpless infant. She gains in attention; she loses out in realizing her potential. Perhaps for all of us there is a seductive pull back to helpless infancy, being cared for, having people anticipate our every wish. Airlines and cruise ships appeal to this desire when they advertise every comfort and luxury their staff will provide if we travel with them. The lucky guest need not lift a finger.

From the description it seems that Laura's natural impulse to do for herself is still strong. When her parents are not in the room she moves around and reaches toys by herself. Yet she doesn't act independently in front of them. She actually becomes more "puffy" when they enter the room. Could it be that she understands already that *for them* she must be helpless? We don't know precisely what Laura understands nor what she gains, but we can guess that this pragmatic child has learned that in some way it is preferable to play up her helplessness and play down her independence. She gets a particular response that she apparently needs. What is certain is that she has learned how to get the kind of attention that the hovering parents are ever-ready to bestow.

As we have seen, children do all kinds of things for parents. They make themselves failures, push themselves to excellence, develop mental and physical symptoms, and relinquish or hang onto their childhood.

They also become our projection screens or mirrors. As mentioned earlier, one of the dangers of projecting parts of ourselves onto our children is that, rather than see and hear *them*, we then respond only to our own reflection. They and their behavior are largely irrelevant to our responses. Regardless of how they behave or how they experience themselves, we don't confirm their reality. Rather we insist that they confirm our reality and relinquish their own. If they are, in any respect, irrelevant to us, they become, in that respect, irrelevant to themselves. What is more, in their eagerness to protect us and give us what we need—our survival means their survival—they often become what we need them to personify for us.

How totally confusing for the child! And how confusing when parents, because of their own internal mixups, blow hot and cold with their child. Fortunately children have enormous flexibility, the ability to ride with the waves and survive. Yet the pain and wounds last a lifetime. Worse, these children will, as we all do, pass onto their children what they have known, perpetuating the disorders through generations. In the interview mentioned earlier Lena Horne twice described herself as having been "cold as ice," the same phrase she used for her mother. She found in herself what she abhorred in her mother.

5 | Contact and Boundaries

Children develop through contact, through relating with others. Consider the normal interaction between a new infant and parents during the course of a day: feeding, diaper changing, holding, carrying, bathing, talking, and singing. These day-by-day shared activities provide the stimulation through which a child develops the capacity to respond physically and emotionally. A baby needs contact, thrives on it, indeed *becomes* on it. Daily contact and response from others support the growth of the new personality; the child becomes more alive and responsive. Or the infant dies a little each day of denied contact. As intellectual stimulation increases the potential use of the brain, so physical and emotional stimulation encourage physical and emotional capacities.

This story was told to me by the adoptive mother of a Korean child who had been deprived of supportive contact and stimulation. At birth the girl had been put in an orphanage and she spent her first four years in several different institutions. Then she was adopted by a Norwegian family with two children of their own. The young adopted daughter did not know how to be in the world, not with adults or with children. She did not look up when her name was called; did she even know her name? She did not respond when the younger child took something from her, but sometimes tears would roll down her expressionless face. Her only response was nonresponse—to withdraw, to sit with a vacant look or to roll up her eyes so that even eye contact was impossible.

This child had had no experience interacting. Relating was unknown to her; she had learned no ways to respond actively to the world. She was almost without a self, an emotional cripple. Her intellectual and physical abilities were also undeveloped. She stumbled when she walked across a room. She didn't talk. Her potential in every area of growth was undeveloped. It was apparent that she had not been touched, physically or emotionally. Twelve years after the adoption the mother told me of her day-by-day struggle to make contact with the child. Months and years of agony and frustration, of concerned care and encouragement, eventually did succeed in counteracting the years of deprivation.

Anywhere people are with people, there is the possibility of interacting in a meaningful way, of having an effect on one another. In families, however, we *know* we have an effect on one another; the interaction is intense, crucial to physical and mental well-being, the very stuff out of which the newly forming personalities are created.

Nourishing contact is "emotional touching." A bond is sensed, even for a split second. A meeting that is meaningful breaks through the isolation of our ordinary existence. The components of the precious and fragile experience that is contact, one person "touching" another, are largely a mystery, yet we all know the experience. We can tell when we are touched and may recognize a moment of contact between others even though no Richter scale can determine when a person has made contact with another or measure the intensity, strength, and duration of the aftershocks of touching.

Sometimes one person may be unaware of the contact or take it for granted. A fifth-grade student showed dramatic improvement in his schoolwork after years of just barely getting by. When his mother asked him what had happened to cause this change he said, "Mr. Brown smiled at me when he passed back the papers."

When Prince Charles of Great Britain married Diana, one observer described the new Princess of Wales this way: "She touches people . . . the old, the young." The speaker went on to explain that people fall in love with Lady Diana because she is interested in them. "She is so open and responsive."

From these two simple examples we glimpse some important features of contact. There is a sense that another sees, hears, and responds to *us*. But these words still leave out the essential ingredient: the *attitude*. It is this that creates part of the mystery of the experience. There is an attitude that conveys the message "I see you, hear you, respond to you, am aware of your existence." In addition to this is the attitude "Your existence doesn't threaten my existence." That is of supreme importance, especially in a family, for when we are not threatened, we can be open to the other.

A child's full development depends on contact, on stimulation, on the encouragement that comes from the attitude "You exist and I validate your existence." What happens when there is contact between parent and child? When the eyes of a baby and parent meet? When a smile is exchanged? A song sung? A back caressed? The interchange is nourishing to the baby in a way that food, by itself, is not. It is indeed food for the soul. From such moments of affinity and relating comes parent/child bonding, a profound and beneficial development.

Contact between people takes place at the boundary between the two. In the physical realm we have little difficulty in locating the boundary. We shake hands, we feel the contact of skin on skin. I know the difference between your hand and my hand. However, it is not always so simple to define our physical boundary. Our senses go beyond the boundaries of our skin. You may feel the warmth of a person's body when you are standing close. You may smell his skin. You can see and hear him across a room. Our voices project out, and with the help of the telephone we can push our boundaries around the world.

If you grew up in a family with brothers and sisters, you may well remember the importance of ownership, defined by boundaries. What was yours and what wasn't was a serious matter. Sharing a room meant there was fierce protection of "my bed," "my bookcase," "my space." But when your brother or sister lay in bed crying, you felt it. The physical boundary between the beds may have been impenetrable, but the emotional boundary was a changing point of emotional contact that moved through space.

Unseen, often unfelt, our emotional boundaries are a point of contact and separation between us and others. They are not a static geographical place or a physical thing. It is important to remember that "boundary" is a convenient metaphor to describe a state of being or stance at a particular moment. Like countries that fear their neighbors will infiltrate their territory, many of us keep our emotional boundaries heavily armed for fear someone will push through and mercilessly take us over. The borders between friendly nations are easily traversed. Likewise, in a friendly context we let others touch us and penetrate our emotional boundaries.

Infants gradually come to separate self from other, me from you; little by little they realize their physical and emotional boundaries and become protective of what belongs to them. Disrespectful parents who assume their children "belong" to them body and soul learn that youngsters will fight for what is theirs. They become shrewd self-protectors when necessary; they shield themselves to ward off parental attempts to emotionally devour them. Their attitude proclaims: "These feelings are mine and you can't have them." They learn to keep everything to themselves. They withhold their smiles as well as their tears; their dreams as well as their feces. A child's last line of defense against overcontrolling, assaultive parents is to take charge of his or her own body functions, which in turn promotes harsher measures like shoving food in one end and enemas in the other. The world is inhabited by countless adults whose natural body functions do not operate without the help of medication.

Our boundaries are penetrable to different degrees at different times with different people. Generally, our early interaction has taught us when it is safe to melt at our boundaries. The Korean girl could be described as being in a fortress; there was no getting through.

The whole realm of emotional contact, the mysterious and intangible happening that occurs between people, is difficult to describe. Sometimes it is closely connected to physical contact. For the very young, the two can't be separated. When a tired toddler climbs up on his father's lap and nestles in, he doesn't separate the warm body feelings from the emotional security. The two are so blended that we talk about "warm feelings," using a physical description for an emotional experience. For the child on his father's lap the smell, the feeling of the shirt, the body warmth, the safety and comfort are all part of Dad.

The child may seem to melt right into his father, yet they are separate people; their skin is the point of physical separation and the point of physical contact between them. Babies are not aware of physical or emotional boundaries. They gradually develop a consciousness of what is their body and what is apart from and outside of their body through touching others and separating from others. A child seems to acknowledge, own, and use parts of himself or herself as they are touched, felt, and defined by others. An extreme case may help to illustrate this.

A friend who works with nursery school children tells of a boy who is the youngest of several children in his family. He was cared for in a barely adequate, desultory fashion with one strange feature: his hands seemed to be totally ignored. He wore hand-me-downs of the older children and his hands were always covered by too-long sleeves. When walking with his mother, she never held his hand. Rather, she would hold the sleeve of his sweater. He was a quiet, shy child who showed little initiative. What is of particular interest is that he almost never used his hands. It was as if he didn't have them available, although physically there was nothing wrong with them. After some therapeutic work with the child and the family to encourage contact the boy showed gradual improvement; he learned to reach out with his hands, to take and to give. He became a more responsive part of the group, both with the other children and the teachers. He learned, literally, to "help himself," at school and at home.

Our capacity to experience and use our emotions depends, like the physical, on contact. Our early relationships enter into our very being to form and define how we experience ourselves and others. Reaching out with our hands to take and to give is the physical equivalent of reaching out emotionally to touch and be touched. In order to do this we must have the capacity to experience our emotions and feelings, and to be aware of boundaries that emotionally separate us from others.

An emotional boundary can be thought of as the point where we connect momentarily and meaningfully with others; the point of meeting. When we have flexible, penetrable boundaries we can reach out and feel with someone, whether it be joy, grief, frustration, or fear—theirs or our own. We take time to feel and register our emotions, rather than rushing to explain them away or beating a quick retreat to neutral topics. We might put into words or express in some other way what we are feeling. We are not threatened by others' existence, nor are we threatened by their feelings, so we can be open to them; we can identify with them. Unlike the Korean child who spent her first four years in institutions, we *dare* to feel and respond. We know when and what we are experiencing, and we show appropriate affect.

When our emotional boundaries are impenetrable, nothing can touch us. We are immune to feelings, our own and others'. "Hardened" and "thick-skinned" are the words that describe such people. It is as if we use our emotional boundaries to shut ourselves off; we neither give nor take. We feel threatened at the possibility of contact. There is no sense of identifying with another, no empathy.

Emotional boundaries are often unclear in families. So closely connected are we that we may lose track of exactly which feelings and emotions belong to whom. What happens to your parents, your brothers or sisters, or your children matters to you, so much so that at times it may seem to happen to you. A mother's sadness becomes her child's sadness. A mother's fear, her child's fear. Parents' boundaries may become extremely penetrable to the point of being nonexistent, making it impossible to separate what is happening to their children from what is happening to them. Mothers have been known to faint in the emergency room of the hospital when their child is being treated. The following story is an example of a mother who identified so completely with her middle-aged son that she could not separate from him.

Stella and her husband, Henry, were visiting her husband's parents. Her mother-in-law phoned long-distance to the younger son, John, and at one point said to Stella, "Would you like to speak to John; he wants to talk to you." Stella felt quite sure that John had not asked to talk to her. For one thing, he had not placed the call. For another, he and Stella had many other opportunities to speak to each other. In addition, there was a quality in her mother-in-law's voice that somehow didn't ring true. She replied, "No, not now, thanks." In a delayed reaction the next morning the mother-in-law complained tearfully to Stella's husband, "How could she not speak to John? And with all he's gone through!" Between the sniffs and sobs it became apparent that *she* felt ignored and rejected. It was as if by not speaking to John, Stella had not spoken to her. Stella, with uncommon maturity and understanding, went over to her mother-in-law, put her arms around her, and reassured her, "We love you, of course we love you," and settled the whole affair.

As is typical in many families, this mother is so involved with her younger son, John, that anything that happens to him happens to her. A slight to him, real or imagined, is a slight to her. Overidentification and confused parent/child boundaries mean confusion for both people. In this family the son has been unable to separate from his parents, and although he is now over forty years old he still is emotionally and financially dependent on them.

Another example of confused boundaries is a parent who can't tolerate hearing the baby cry. So complete is the identification, so nonexistent the emotional boundaries, that the parent wants to cry, too. Such parents do anything to keep their baby from crying, often resulting in a tyrannical child.

Such close identification makes good contact impossible, for only when there is a clear difference between what is you and what is not you can you experience a meeting between the two. If the water in the tub is the same temperature as your body, you won't feel the water. When it is colder or warmer, the contact is experienced. If you hold hands with another without moving over a period of time—for instance, lying in bed— you may lose the sensation of touching. Only through moving do you again experience the difference between your hand and the other's, and the contact between the two.

Identifying with others, having empathy—the ability to feel with them—along with clear emotional boundaries makes good contact possible. Yet when the identification is complete to the point of confluence, of blending in with another, then we lose the reality of separateness between the two. For children it is of vital importance that they are responded to, not as clones, or as extensions of parents, but as separate individuals.

As we have discussed in earlier chapters, for some parents having children who differ from them seems threatening. Differences in the realm of feelings and emotions may make parents especially uneasy. The parents, for their own protection, then attempt to create the child in their own image, with the same emotional range and intensity, thereby assuring their own safety and, unfortunately, little contact as well.

Satisfaction in our interactions with others comes with good contact. Good contact does not necessarily mean a profound meeting or deep emotional touching. When there is listening, hearing, and responding in our everyday interaction with others, we part feeling acknowledged, recognized as worthwhile. Let's imagine such a scene:

Child: Can I go over to Jerry's house to play?
Mother: No. You remember we agreed that on school days you have to stay home after supper.
Child: Yeah, I know, but since we finished supper early and all my homework is done, I thought maybe you'd make an exception.
Mother: I hear all your reasons and they sound good, but I'm afraid, somehow, to start making exceptions.
Child: (Pleading) Please?
Mother: No. I know you're disappointed, and I'm sorry. My decision is no. I'm just about to put the cookies on a tin to bake. Do you want to help?
Child: I don't even want to *eat* any of your dumb cookies. (He leaves the room.)

A few minutes later as the smell of cookies permeates the house:

Child: O.K. I'll eat a cookie. When will they be ready? (He picks up a spoon and helps put dough on another tin. He talks about other things with his mother.)

And life continues. Let us imagine a scene without contact. The child makes the same request.

Child: Can I go over to Jerry's house to play?
(Mother is busy and doesn't answer. The child asks again.)
Mother: (Without looking up) Uh-uh.

Child: (Gives reasons, switches to a whiny voice.)
Mother: Stop whining.
Child: (Pouting) Pleeaase can I go?
Mother: (In an angry voice) I said no. You just can't take no for an answer.

The child argues a little more, Mother's anger mounts. Just at the point before she loses all control, the child stomps out and slams the door. The mother is left with unexpressed anger, the child with unexpressed hostility.

No one gets any satisfaction in this example. Mother is impermeable to her child. She is not going to be touched. From the outset she doesn't look or listen. Then she accuses, "You just can't take no for an answer." To appreciate this response and this mother, we must hear what her mother has said about her when she was a child. "She really knew her own mind; *she never could take no for an answer.*" This is an amazing coincidence. What's more, when the husband talks about his wife, we hear the very same words: "She can't take no for an answer." This is surely more than a coincidence. The husband adds, "And our son is just like his mother."

This shared characteristic is not simply a "family resemblance" or a coincidence. It's like a hot potato that no one wants and tosses to the nearest person. Mother obviously got it from her mother when she was a youngster. It may have been a "family heirloom" even then. "She's just like her aunt Marie. She never could take no for an answer." Obvious from the tone of voice was that this was not a good way to be. Then she grew up and had a son: a place to toss the hot potato.

Mother tosses the description at her son at the point

when he in some way begins to threaten her existence. How does he do that? By reminding her of herself at an earlier time. She is on the verge of feeling like a youngster again, and creeping to the edge of her consciousness is the fear and rejection she felt in relation to her mother. Her son's existence in that moment of identifying with him is a threat to her existence. Thrown off her equilibrium, she hardens herself and defends her emotional boundaries against "invasion" by the leftovers from her childhood. This requires that she use the most effective tactic, her ever-ready protection; that is, to become like the parent she knew so long ago, impatient and angry. All done in a split second, with no conscious thought. In hardening herself against her old pain, she has hardened herself against her son.

In the instant that the threat falls over her, she reinforces her boundaries; she rejects any identification with him. Rather she identifies with her mother, using her words of accusation. To identify with the power of a parent is more comfortable than to identify with the impotence and bad feelings of being an accused child. She says the same words her mother said to her, in the same voice, with the same negative tone. She becomes her mother; not really, of course, but the internalized negative mother, also called the "introjected" mother.

Just at the time when the mother might have seen her son, maybe have been touched by him, identified with him, and responded, at that point she put up an impermeable boundary. Tender spots guard against being touched again. It is as if she staves off any contact between her and her son. With those magic words, "You just won't take no for an answer," those negative qualities that are internalized from her mother take over. The interaction becomes programmed; he pushes his mother's buttons and she unwittingly encourages in her son the very behavior that sets her off. This is the dance that is repeated over and over between child and Mother. They provide their own music, neither misses a beat.

If Mother took a breath, blinked her eyes, and really saw her son, she might react in a different, more responsive way to him and the situation at the moment. But she is in a kind of trance. She is being "automatic mother." When she hears, "Mother, can I . . . ?" she utters, "Uh-uh." Typically, most of our automatic reactions, those words and actions that seem to originate not from our conscious self but from some internal tape, are our way to stay out of contact in what seems like a potentially threatening situation.

Parents with hardened emotional boundaries find it difficult, if not impossible, to emotionally touch and be touched by their children. A child cries with disappointment, screams in frustration or fear, or even giggles with delight and the parent reacts with a severe look, a harsh word, or a slap that informs: "Stifle that expression." With each such experience a child becomes a little less spontaneous, a little less expressive. He or she loses the ability to experience purely and freely, and to talk about the experience. The bruised emotional boundary heals, but a reinforced fence goes up at that point to protect what becomes a susceptible point.

There seems to be a connection between how threatened a parent feels by the child's experience or expression and how strong is the parent's reaction. Another way to put this is, If you have a powerfully harsh parent running around inside you, ready to commandeer at any moment, the more threatened you will be by your child. The incident of the child who said he couldn't do his homework illustrates this. His mother lost all control. As she told it, "I hit him as hard as I could." Like an animal ready to spring and devour, the parent inside grabbed control. The mother couldn't stop herself. This was obviously a very tender spot for her.

The harsh parent inside is called the internalized or introjected parent, and this example affirms what is known of introjects. According to Genie Laborde in her doctoral dissertation on that subject, introjects, first, do not allow for options. The mother did not have a choice. As she said, she lost all control. Second, introjects operate in response to certain stimuli, in this case, the boy repeating, "I can't get it." The situation may vary, but a certain stimulus must be present. Third, introjects are always unconscious.

Parents who carry the heavy burden of unresolved grief are especially affected by a child's crying, as discussed earlier in the case of the mother who brutalized her infant. A parent's unresolved grief, compounded by life's frustrations, is undoubtedly behind much physical abuse of children. A mother will say to explain away her harsh beating of her child, "She started to cry and I couldn't stand her crying." Or a father's explanation, "I wanted to teach him not to cry."

Parents who haven't acknowledged and expressed their grief will frequently feel so tender that they erect impenetrable walls around themselves. They become vacant and unresponsive. This can happen when parents themselves have lost their parents and have been unable to separate from them in a clear way. Let's look at such a situation. Joan spent her life trying to please her mother. Every visit was fraught with tension, whether Joan visited her mother or her mother came to her. Joan did not weep at her mother's funeral. She and her husband made all the arrangements, took care of her mother's personal belongings, and went on with life— or so it seemed on the surface. Shortly after Joan's mother died, Joan was pleased to discover she was pregnant. When their son was born Joan and her husband named him Mark, not too different from Joan's mother's name, Martha. It was neither their family's nor their religion's tradition to do so. Was she aware of the similarity in names? Mark was a lively baby with a lusty cry. From the very first days in the hospital Joan found it extremely upsetting when he cried. At home she had two different reactions. Sometimes she would watch and feel untouched as he lay in his crib and screamed, almost as if she were watching a film that had nothing to do with her. Other times she wanted to kill him when he cried. She had to separate herself from the sound, close every door between them, and turn on the radio to full volume. Joan took care of the obvious needs of her baby, but was generally distracted, as if the baby were not as real as her inner thoughts, although if you asked her she really couldn't tell you what her inner thoughts were.

Mark learned, as all children do, how his mother was available to him and how she was not. He, too, developed an inner world, and as a nursery school boy he was described as a loner and a dreamer. The teachers couldn't contact him, yet there were other times when he clung to them. Through his school years he was slow and unresponsive. Finally he could no longer attend school; he was considered disturbed, depressed, in need of therapy.

A recent study by Froma W. Walsh of three groups of families sheds some light on the connection between bereaved parents and their children. In the first group were families with a diagnosed schizophrenic child; in the second group, families with a depressed child; and in the third group, those with so-called "normal children." It was found that in group I, the families with a schizophrenic child, there had been an extremely high number of grandparent deaths within a period of one year before to one year after the birth of the child. In group II, the families with a depressed child, the number was lower, and in group III, the families with a normal child, the number of grandparent deaths was low. This in itself could simply be coincidence, but there was strong evidence that the deaths in groups I and II were not grieved for. Even after fourteen years or more, there was great difficulty for some of the families in talking about the grandparent who had died and about the actual death itself. These parents never truly separated from their own parents, never went through the grieving process, and could not then make good contact with their own children.

Since contact depends on seeing, hearing, and responding to another, those family situations that interfere with such interaction are important to identify. One area frequently muddled in family relationships is the confusion among various generations. For example, a mother might confuse her daughter with her mother; that is, the child's grandmother. A young woman complained to me about her mother: "She's very demanding; she thinks I never do anything right. She's never satisfied." This was followed by complaints about her daughter—the same complaints exactly, voiced in the same way. Her daughter was four years old.

This brief description shows how a parent re-created with her daughter the identical relationship she had with her mother. She reinvented her mother in her daughter. In such cases the contact between parent and child is bound to be poor. The parent responds not to the child as a unique individual, but instead is thrown back to his or her own childhood relationship with the older generation. As the parent was intimidated by her mother, so she is intimidated by her child. Feelings of intimidation are not conducive to contact.

A father tells of his emotional mix-up with his son in contrast to the clarity he has with his daughter. With her he is patient and kind. They have good contact; he sees her and responds to her, she doesn't threaten his existence. As he talks about his son, however, he starts to cry in the telling. With his son, he is just like his father was with him, harsh and impatient. He identifies so closely with his son that each small indication that his son is afraid, angry, or vulnerable in any way brings the father back to all the old fears and feelings of impotence of his childhood. The boundaries between them disappear in an instant. To protect those tender spots the father puts up a wall, and the ghost of *his* father takes over.

Good contact between a parent and child does not always mean sweet and nice interaction. Emotional responses are not rehearsed or planned; they are spontaneous reactions to a thought, a situation, a person, as diverse as bursting into laughter at a joke or into tears at a movie. Parents may have extremely angry or impatient responses that have nothing to do with their childhood and everything to do with the real child at that very moment. A spontaneous response in anger also lets a child know that he or she exists, that he or she is being taken seriously. If, however, your spontaneous responses mean that you lose touch with your child and lose control of your actions, that you later say with remorse, "I wasn't myself," then you may be sure you are acting out of a program from the tape of the introjected parent.

Here is a unique success story of desperate parents at the end of their rope, who in an unusual way let their daughter know they truly saw her. In talking about their daughter, the parents described her as having been a bright, cooperative girl, a fine big sister to the three younger children. Suddenly their daughter hit thirteen and a demon seemed to take over. The parents said to themselves, "So this is the terrible teens," and felt helpless and generally hopeless, too. They literally did not know what to do. After some months they began to wonder whether they would survive. The mother happened to be program chairman for the P.T.A., and she figured that other parents must feel as ineffective as she and her husband did. Perhaps she could plan a program that would help solve the problem of what to do with the little monsters. Creative and determined, she found in the library a play with a character very similar to her daughter. She went to the drama department of the local university and asked whether they would be willing to perform this play for the P.T.A.s in the city. They agreed to do it.

The thirteen-year-old daughter was aware of the plan

and asked whether she could play the role of the teen-ager. And so the event took place. Before 450 people, the girl played the terrible teen. After the performance the audience divided into small groups to discuss the play and how it touched them. The girl, meanwhile, sat by herself, waiting for her folks to give her a ride home. She saw all those people discussing *her*. Indeed she had been seen and heard and taken seriously. She was not a threat to the audience's existence; after all, it was only a play. When the parents at last got in the car with her to drive home she seemed somehow subdued. And as her father said, "The monster was gone and we had our daughter again."

Children long to be seen and heard, to have their existence validated. They do what they can to elicit some concern, some response to *them*. Like all of us, they resent being mistaken for someone else, the person they "used to" be, the person they "should" be, or a parent or grandparent. Sometimes parents say, "I don't know what I did, but I finally got through. Now things are going much smoother." When we get through it means our boundaries are clear, we are in contact with ourselves and with our child, and the child gets the message clearly.

Paradoxically, the experience of being seen, heard, and responded to—the act of contact—makes separation possible. When there has been no meeting, there can be no separation. As Philip Kennard wrote in his song "Survivor," "Never together means never apart, it's not the end 'cause we never did start." We dare to experience connection only when we trust ourselves to be able to handle loss. As infants we do it all naturally. The meetings with the mother are total connection; the partings—being left in the crib, for instance—are accompanied by crying loudly, grieving for the loss. That experience of crying with your whole being in some way helps resolve the loss. (Recent research suggests that emotional crying, in contrast to tears from peeling onions, actually rids the body of certain toxins.) When the mother leaves too often or for too long, the child may not handle the separations so well. No response to his crying from Mother leads to a gradual giving up. The grieving doesn't get finished up and the contact isn't as total as it once was.

Separation between parent and child is a gradual process that begins at birth with the cutting of the umbilical cord and continues as a normal part of the physical and emotional growth of the child. In *Catharsis in Healing, Ritual, and Drama*, T. J. Scheff brings to attention the ancient and beloved game of peek-a-boo as a step in the process of parting, a symbolic and controlled way to play at saying goodbye and coming back again. With each coming together, each moment of contact, there is the knowledge of possible parting and loss. When Mother or Father stays away too long, peek-a-boo is no longer fun. Laughter changes to tears.

The process of parent and child having more and more physical and emotional separation is a natural part of the individuation of the child. He or she becomes more of an independent person, taking steps to move out into the world. All kids have a strong desire to do this. But this natural process of contact and separation doesn't always go smoothly. There is an inherent conflict of interests. How hard it is for us parents to trust our young ones, to stay out of their way, to let them go. We get so mixed up when our fears from our early years are reawakened with our child's development. We remember our own growing pains and want so much to protect them, even when we know they must learn their own lessons.

Nursery school, first grade, the teens, and college—the leaving-home times are often the times of crisis, precarious junctures in the life of a family. Our efforts to protect our young are efforts to protect ourselves, as well. Take the first day at nursery school, for example. We see a look of some apprehension in our child's eye. All our fears are reactivated. Memories flood in from the time we took our first steps away from home. Will I make it? Who will take care of me? Will anyone play with me? Will the teachers be kind to me? Will I do something wrong? When will Mommy come back? Our children have their own misgivings. Surely it is not only our generation that was so fearful! Our job, then, is to listen and hear what our child is saying and respond; to recognize our own unfinished business and how we are influenced by it. When our residual fears seize and blind so that we blend into our child's experience, we can't make contact. The child's needs are neglected.

This may be the most difficult aspect of being a parent: to listen to the child, acknowledge that he or she has problems and fears, or perhaps does *not* have problem and fears, and trust that he or she will cope and survive—and so will we. To do this we have to know for certain that we and our children are separate people. We have our own problems and fears that we have to cope with and they have theirs. As soon as we mix ourselves up with our children we respond to a part of ourselves and the children get lost again.

We usually interweave ourselves with our children, to

protect them or, subconsciously, to protect ourselves. Overinvolvement makes separation impossible. We explain our solicitude and our overinvestment with our kids in terms of *their* needs. "He's so afraid of dogs he can't go out without me." "She really isn't up to going to nursery school; she gets so wrought up playing with other children." "I never went to kindergarten and I think six is young enough to go to school. They don't learn anything there anyway." We keep secret from ourselves the fact that it is we who are clinging to our children, but they, like eight-month-old Laura, catch on early. They absorb our attitudes, and when they realize that their development is a threat to us, they interrupt their growth for us. They become fearful of new situations. They even become allergic and phobic, developing physical symptoms to stay out of school.

Confused boundaries again. Who needs whom? Who is doing what to whom? For whom? Whose fears? Whose phobias? As soon as the child gets involved in the emotional needs of the parent, the necessary ingredients for good contact are gone. Parent and child can't see, hear, respond to one another as separate individuals with the attitude "Your existence doesn't threaten my existence." The parents are threatened by growth toward independence, as in the case of Laura. Laura is threatened when she feels her parents' need that she be helpless. Growth and independence, both integral parts of the process of becoming whole, are curtailed, in the child and in the parent. Parent and child are caught in a clinch, close but with no contact, overinvolved with each other, emotionally enmeshed—stunted.

A common symptom of disturbance in a family is a child who doesn't leave home. He or she stays long after the time of expected departure, although neither parents nor child claim to like the arrangement very much. Some kids are on the verge of leaving for years and never quite make it: the expected job doesn't materialize, the final six credits at college are never completed, the jobs around the house aren't finished. There are always reasons. What are they waiting for? What do they want?

Some wait for that moment when they feel acknowledged by their parents, accepted for who they are, separate, worthwhile individuals. They wait for the day their parents will say, "You're a free person. We are proud of you and will always be glad to see you. Now go." The dream of the parents' acceptance and love, paradoxically, keeps their children at home, often in a disagreeable situation. If they leave, they may never get what they want.

Others stay to serve their parents in some way, to provide the love, acceptance, and companionship the parents don't get elsewhere. Or they stay to stabilize their parents' marriage. Children cling to parents and thus avoid growing up and becoming adults. This may also be for the parents' sake. If the child never grows up, the parents never grow old. Of course parents grow old anyway, yet we must remember that the emotional influences on our behavior do not have to satisfy our logical minds. Each of us knows better than to think we can solve our parents' problems. But how many of us have spent our lives trying? As parents, we try to solve our children's problems. That doesn't work, either.

The game of peek-a-boo is fun. It is a prescribed parting, only to meet again at the right moment: two seconds, five seconds, or a wonderfully frightening and agonizing ten seconds later. Both parent and baby know the rules. If they depart from the rules the game is no fun. Emotional separation between parent and child is another story, often involving fear and agony for longer than ten seconds. When little Jane goes off to school for the first time, or big Jane goes to work in a faraway city, Mother "feels" with her daughter all the mixed emotions that accompany any big new step. To identify with and feel with another is marvelous, especially for a parent and child. Those closely shared feelings are a special part of the bond between people. But we parents are walking on thin ice when we cannot discriminate that which remains from our childhood, those unfinished concerns and desires that are activated by our child's normal steps through life, from the present-day situation in our child's life. Our emotional relics send us right through the crack in the ice into chilly waters and we grasp for those we pull right down with us—our children.

6 | The Family System

A couple talks in private about getting a divorce. Their daughter, age one, starts having nightmares.

"Every time her daughter is in town she starts drinking," remarks a woman about her friend.

Among a group of Amazon Indians there is a saying that a daughter who is overthin is too connected to her father.

Family ties are unlike any other connections. Invisible, complex, powerful beyond words, like marionette strings they move us in ways we cannot begin to fathom. They tug at us from eight thousand miles away, pull at our emotions, and influence our behavior for our entire lives. Here is a comment of a 77-year-old woman about her 81-year-old sister, with the total agreement of the oldest sister, age 86: "We always call her 'Miss Have Not.' That's because she's the middle daughter." One can imagine that comment was made for the first time more than seventy years before, and repeated a few thousand times since then.

What goes on between people in a family—husband and wife, parents and children, brothers and sisters, grandparents and grandchildren—is part of the family system, the large tapestry that weaves in the past and the present, and includes all members of the family, even those who live only in our memory.

We are all born into a social system. Although a single parent and one child make a system, such a dyad is still part of a larger system. The absent father, living elsewhere or even dead, is rarely completely out of the picture, but remains to exert influence. Frequently a third person lives in the household, a boyfriend or girlfriend, temporarily or long term. Even when the parent's friends are determined to keep hands off child rearing, those people are part of the system. A grandparent might be on the scene, either in reality or prevailing in the mind and heart of the parent. Perhaps members of a communal household compose the larger system.

The 'family system' refers to the members of the household and anyone, present or not, who exerts constant influence on patterns of family interaction. A young man told of being compared in every aspect of life with a brother who died before he was born. The dead brother remained a part of the system. In another family the grandfather who lived two thousand miles away was part of the system. He was the source of money and called the shots.

The context of the family system is significant when

we consider the development of a child or when we take an interest in how the individuals function in our family. Each member of the system has a part to play in the system, one or more primary roles to perform: these roles, sometimes handed down from one generation to the next, frequently become the life script of a person. Sheldon Kopp, a psychiatrist and author, in his book *This Side of Tragedy*, writes that his role was chosen for him before he was born: "I myself was cast at conception as the villain." He adds, "From the start I made my mother nervous, gave her pain, and endangered her very life." A book about alcoholic families, Sharon Wegscheider's *Another Chance: Hope and Health for the Alcoholic Family*, points to the typical roles in such families and to the persons who generally take them on: the enabler, the hero, the scapegoat, the lost child, and the mascot.

The family system is made up of people, and although we tend to speak of it as if it has life, power, and needs of its own, it is only what the family members make it. At the same time, one of the characteristics of a system is that it is more than the sum of its parts. We may think about "the government," for example, as if it were separate from the individuals who make up the government and those of us who elect them to positions of power. "The government doesn't pay any attention to the little man." Or "The city doesn't do anything about fixing the roads." We say, "My family wouldn't allow me to talk like that." Those who work with family systems often make such statements as "The family system will do what is necessary to maintain itself." This kind of talk can make us feel helpless in the face of the system. The fact is we create a system to provide what we need for our survival and the survival of the species, the same as bees or ants do. Through the family system we ensure these basics of life to the members: shelter, food, protection, and especially connection with others.

We individuals are the ones who preserve our family system. We keep track of each other. We make sure people come home at night, or, if they don't, we know where they are. We encourage holidays together. We send photos and call on the phone when we're away. In some tragic cases, families fall apart, parents die or form new units, children are separated from parents and brothers and sisters, never to connect again. Some, as we read in the newspaper, find each other after forty years and come together in tearful reunions.

It takes an effort, especially in difficult times, to maintain the family system, yet we all know cases of extreme hardship where family members put the good of the system before their own personal gain. Each of us does what we presume is necessary to make the system work, taking on roles to carry out the essential functions of the system. Somebody provides money for necessities. Somebody brings in food. Somebody takes out the garbage. In addition, there are those psychological and emotional roles that are not so explicit or obvious, those that are useful for the special workings of that particular system, those we assume over time from the encouragement of other members. An example is Sheldon Kopp's statement above that he was cast as the villain. He goes on to tell that his sister was "miscast" temporarily as the "flawless dream child," until he left home and "they began recasting her to take a revised version of my role."

Negative roles, such as "bad kid," can balance a system and keep a family intact. Sometimes the roles are handed down from generation to generation to continue a particular interplay between family members. In his book *The Politics of the Family*, R. D. Laing relates his visit to the family of "David," a "possible schizophrenic" according to a recent medical diagnosis:

> We can just glimpse in this family a drama perpetuated over three generations—the players are two women and a man: first, mother, daughter, and father; second, mother, daughter, and daughter's son. Daughter's father dies—daughter conceives a son, *to replace* her father. The play's the thing. The actors come and go. As they die, others are born. The new-born enters the part vacated by the newly dead.

We tend to find what we are looking for in our children's behavior. We describe and define, and sure enough we find. What we conceive we perceive. David's mother and grandmother found him to be "just like" his grandfather. So they perceived him. So they described him, repeatedly. So he became, on the surface, not to disappoint them. Even if it was driving him "crazy." Children become what parents need them to be. The process is gradual and sure. After all, families, have time and proximity in their favor.

"No trouble from you, I've got enough with your brother." That remark, repeated over time, could give rise to the roles of good kid and bad kid. Father wants a little attention, daughter rubs his back and listens to his problems when Mother is busy elsewhere. With some encouragement from Dad and cooperation from

Mother, daughter might be induced to take as her role substitute wife, as if by ministering to Dad's needs, she can keep him happy and at home.

Whether the roles become rigid patterns depends on the flexibility of the system, how readily the individuals can alter the steps of their dance. In a flexible system, if the father is unable to bring in the money, the role of provider is taken over by the mother, the oldest child, or the state. In an inflexible system, no one but Dad can do that job. Everyone supports the familiar arrangement, protecting Dad's needs for top position and the others' needs for submissive positions. When the system is immobilized—no money, no food—the suffering becomes extreme. Then somebody may break out of the rules of the system or, more likely, an outside person or agency moves in to change the system.

Nobody wakes up in the morning thinking, "I wonder what our system needs today." Yet through our actions and our interactions we create and sustain the larger whole, our family system. We are flexible and change rules, or we are resolute in keeping the rules and behavior static. When people sense that their system is shaky, they get more repetitive in their interaction and more extreme in their actions. Fear propels us into various attempts to preserve what we have, seemingly at all costs. Much family research in the last twenty years has pointed up the sacrifices that children make, the extremes to which they will go, to take on the role of family savior.

To an observer, the role may seem only destructive: to remain a baby, to pretend to be happy all the time, to become Mother's confidant, to get addicted to drugs, to abuse alcohol, to come down with psychosomatic problems, to get pregnant at age 15. To those who treat families, all can be seen also as misguided attempts to keep the family system together. We play our roles, usually without realizing it, without defining what we are doing as helping to sustain our system, and always we do so with the cooperation of the others. We simply live our lives in relation to other family members in our usual ways from day to day, unconscious of how we live and act at the system level.

Looking at the family as a system is like looking at family interaction on a new level. Imagine you look through the roof of a house to the levels below. The upper story is easy to perceive; that is analogous to the communication level of family interaction. You hear what family members say to each other. You see who interacts with whom. The level below isn't so clear at first glance. If you look with a trained eye at that level, a complex and fascinating scene emerges. You are witness to the inner workings, the machinery—the family system. You see how the rules are made, some in conscious moments of careful deliberation, others evolving over time. You see who takes each of the various roles, which roles are interchangeable, which interactions are repeated without alteration over time. You see how this group of people keeps itself functioning. In short, you see the operation of the family system.

Interest in the family as a system has exploded in the last few decades. Many questions and problems that had previously stumped the experts can now be understood more clearly with this new perspective. How did it happen, for instance, that when one of a couple stopped drinking the other one became an alcoholic? How to explain that one child in a family excelled in school and in life while another, apparently of equal intelligence, became a drop-out and a drug addict? Why do various therapeutic approaches with different members of a family not equally alleviate the pain in the family members or increase their ability to function?

What was startling was this: behavior that seemed unproductive to family members, even obviously damaging, served an important function at the family system level. Behavior that on the surface made no sense at all made lots of sense at the system level. Consider this situation: a woman constantly defers to her husband, credits him with achievements that are actually hers, eagerly strips herself of any personal power. She apparently behaves in a self-defeating manner. At the system level, however, she takes an essential role, one that balances those of her husband and children. *A role in a system is never sustained by a single person but only by the collaboration of all members of the system.* A child of five who refuses to be toilet trained does so only with the tacit cooperation of the parents.

To understand the family system and its importance in making sense out of what we do in our families, we must look briefly at what a human system is. What makes a group of people more than just a group of people? What makes them a system? One of the givens of any system is *rules*. There are rules in the family system, rules that govern who is part of the system and who isn't, how people behave in this particular system, how they are punished if they misbehave, how the system interacts with the rest of the world. Any group of people who interact over time, even a short period of time, must create rules for their behavior. Some rules are explicit and negotiated, others are implicit, never conscious, never talked about.

One of the first rules to be decided is who is in charge. When the electricity went out in New York City some years ago, in each group there was one person who emerged as leader. One such man described how he led the workers who shared his office down the pitch black corridor to the stairwell, how they crept down the stairs, all thirty-six flights—he took it upon himself to keep careful count—and how he then headed for the main door out to the street. Much to his surprise the door wasn't where it was supposed to be. "The thirteenth floor, of course, there is no thirteenth floor," said another, who promptly took charge of calming the others down. Then he somehow got the group turned around, the former leader at the tail end, and proceeded up out of the basement, on to the ground level, and out the door.

In a healthy family system the parents are chief administrators. They are in charge. As children grow they may become authorities in various activities—which new piece of electronic equipment to buy, where the best fishing places are to be found. But the parents are in charge. When children take over in any area of family functioning, and as we know they do in many cases, it must always be with a nod of the head of one or both of the parents.

This also holds true in single-parent families, when other complications arise as well. A teenager living with her father gets into a struggle over drugs, dating, and school attendance. Mother is not on the scene, but she is part of the old familiar system, supporting her daughter against the father at every opportunity. Mother

agrees with Father that daughter should not take drugs:
at the same time she complains to daughter how
"straight" Father is. How could she ever have been married to such a man?

A single mother complained that her son of six was
getting in her bed during the night. He also had taken
charge of his bedtime, making her sit with him until he
fell asleep. "Even when I have something important to
do, he won't let me." In this case there was no father on
the scene in cahoots with the son. In fact, when the
parents were together, Father complained to Mother
about their son getting in her bed. This is an example of
Mother taking two roles. On the one hand she scolds
her son for getting into her bed during the night and for
not going to sleep promptly when she puts him to bed.
On the other hand, she remembers when she was a
child, afraid to be in the dark room by herself, crying
herself to sleep, no one coming to her. In this respect
she has lost the boundaries between her and her son.
She indulges her son since her identification with him is
so intense that to refuse him her company at night is
like refusing herself. As a point of interest, when the
boy is with his father he also sleeps in the same bed
with him. Both parents show ambivalence on the issue
although when they lived together they took opposite
sides on the issue.

For a single parent to be in charge, he or she must be
of a single mind. Otherwise the child takes over in the
same way as when one parent shakes his head, "No,"
and the other nods, "Yes."

Parents who relinquish their authority are in deep
trouble. They themselves eventually wonder, How did
it happen, how have we allowed this child to terrorize

me? Or us? How could it come about that the daughter took over the kitchen and would not let anyone else in, even her mother, to prepare a meal? In some families the six-month-old infant already rules the roost. How could that happen?

Systems have boundaries, both physical and emotional. Usually one or both parents function as "gatekeepers"; they make the rules about who can enter and who stays out. This is frequently a point of contention between a pair. One says, "We never see anybody. Why can't we have more people over?" The other says, "I don't want a lot of strangers traipsing through here." Mothers are frequently explicit gatekeepers: "Check with me before you invite friends over." Who goes out, when, and for how long is also carefully watched in family systems. For some it may be a threat to the system for Mother to go out to work. What foreign influence might she bring back with her? Does Father go out to a ballgame? Does the daughter go out after dark?

In addition to who comes and goes, gatekeepers watch for what comes and goes. No girlie magazines, no subversive literature, no hard rock music may come over this threshold! What may not go out? Family secrets, money issues, special family belongings that are not to be lent.

Many system rules are not made explicit; in fact, more often than not those rules that govern the system and interaction between members of the system are conveyed nonverbally. Yet, within the family, everyone knows the rules. In some families any intimacy outside the family is against the rules. All emotions are to be expressed inside the home. In other families no emotion is expressed at home. In an autobiographical piece by

Colette she tells of returning with her family from a day in the country: ". . . no doubt we looked very happy, since to look happy was the highest compliment we paid each other." This comment suggests they had the rule shared by many families: in front of others we must look happy.

Some rules regulate feelings, emotions, touching one another either in anger or affection. We create rules in our family system that prescribe what we should see as well as what can be talked about. Rules determine roles. Who is rulemaker? Who can break the rules? Who can be competent? Who stays helpless? Who can be more competent than whom? Who can clown around and who must be serious?

All of the interaction that goes on in the family both creates the rules and roles and is a manifestation of the rules and roles. Here is a simplified example of a scene at the dinner table that illustrates this point:

Mother: (Sitting down at the table) Let's have no bickering at the table tonight.
Child #1: It's always Johnny who starts it.
Child #2: (Elbow in ribs of child #1) Shut up. I do not.
Mother: Please! Here we go again. (To Father) Will you please do something?
Father: Johnny, leave the table.

By the way that Mother begins the conversation we know that bickering at the table is the usual fare and, in a subtle way, that Mother incites it. There are ways of saying "Don't" that come out sounding like "Do." We see that child #1 is a troublemaker who blames the other. Johnny plays his part to perfection, denying and at the same time escalating the action, punctuating with the elbow. Mother comes in again with her helplessness and calls in Father. Father comes out of his reverie, takes action, and gets rid of Johnny.

What would happen if one member should step out of role? Who would try to put him or her back in? How? Would everyone join in to try to keep the familiar interaction or is that the job of one person? How does the "bad" child behave when the "good" child steps out of line? Who feels the most anxiety when the usual patterns are upset?

We take our rules and roles so much for granted that we rarely talk about or question them, either as children or adults. Young children do, but they are swiftly discouraged. For example, this was told to me by a mother of two children, Johnny, 9, and Kathy, 12. Kathy is practicing the piano:

Kathy: Mother, how come Johnny can make mistakes and I can't?
Mother: What do you mean?
Kathy: Well, when Johnny makes a mistake you say, "That's very nice, dear, why don't you play it again." When I make a mistake you yell at me.

Children grow and their world broadens. They visit friends and relatives, and notice that other families do things differently. They come home with all kinds of ideas. "Why can't we do it like they do at Joanne's house? They watch TV while they eat." "That's not the way we do it here." In such exchanges rules are made clear. We do or don't do in our families according to the ways of our system.

Family mythology plays an important part in any family system. It tells us how to see and to explain what goes on, what and whom we are to worry about, how we got to be the way we are: rich, poor, troubled, crazy, or whatever. A family with four daughters came for counseling. One of the rules of this family was that members were to be nice to one another. The parents set the example. They didn't fight. Despite the rule, the two youngest girls quarreled incessantly. The reasons for the girls' quarreling were agreed upon by all of the family members. This was the story: Shortly after daughter #4 was born, daughter #3 became seriously ill and spent some time in the hospital. Much of the parents' time and energy was focused on the older sister. Because of this, the younger daughter harbored resentments; thus the fighting.

These two girls were now ten and twelve. The question was, What function did the girls' quarreling serve in the system and how was it reinforced? The youngest daughter and her father sat beside each other during the session. They touched each other almost constantly, much of the time making contact with their feet, sometimes one or the other reaching out a hand to the other. The next older girl sat beside her mother. They often exchanged glances and nodded in agreement when one or the other spoke. There seemed to be two couples: Father and the youngest girl, Mother and the next older girl. The two older girls participated little in the interaction, although the mother had first called for help because of her concern with the oldest. Whenever the younger girls sensed that their parents might disagree they started quarreling. They were the seconds fighting the duel for the combatants who never picked up their pistols, took their positions, and fought it out themselves. The function of the quarreling became clear. It was reinforced partly by the mythology. The family all accepted an event in the past as the reason why the girls were behaving a certain way now. Since they could not change the past event, it followed they could not change present behavior. Secondly, each parent reinforced the girls' quarreling by recruiting one daughter to do his or her dirty work.

The mother later called me for a separate appointment. Her issue was this: she was concerned that her husband might be having an affair. This was similar to the worry she had expressed. She had never spoken to him about it, couldn't believe that he would actually do so, but she needed to tell someone. When the parents came for an appointment together she criticized him, always in a pleasant tone of voice, about one thing or another, and he calmly explained himself and his actions. Never were her suspicions mentioned. Never did they get angry or quarrel. Neither had any direct way to assert himself or herself. They seemed relieved when they were encouraged to talk straight to one another, to stop hiding out and pussy-footing around. Soon after, the parents reported that they had quarreled and survived, that the younger girls had stopped their incessant quarreling and even played together from time to time. When asked about her husband's "affair" the wife brushed off the question. "Oh, I don't worry about that anymore."

The family mythology portrayed a happy couple who had no problems. How much safer for the perpetuation of the family system to have two little girls quarrel than to have the parents bring their differences out in the open.

One of the axioms of a family system is that whatever one member does affects the other members: we are all affected by each other. The following quotation comes from Carl Whitaker, a well-known family therapist:

> I was treating a woman who was a bad alcoholic, and her husband was very indignant about coming in. He had five years of analysis and he certainly didn't need any more help! After six months or so came Christmas time and she arrived at the decision not to drink. For the first weekend in several years since they had been married she didn't touch a drop. The next week hubby tossed away a fifth and a half in two days and a half, which was better than Mama had ever done.

The family with four daughters and the drinking couple have something in common. By their behavior, they were keeping a balance in the family system. Though they had some pain, they did not have chaos. In each case the most important rule of the system was being followed: *keep this system from falling apart*. It is certain that the husband who started to drink when his wife quit did not consciously think of regaining the balance that was upset when his wife gave up alcohol. Nor did the little girls in the family consciously decide to quarrel or to stop quarreling. They simply reacted to the demands, as they perceived them, to save their family system—the same as we all do.

Our family system has profound significance for each

of us. Consciously or unconsciously, we do what we are able to keep it intact. In this way, we avoid the chaos that threatens if the system should fall apart. We resist the emotion that is certain to result from no connections—the anomie that leaves us disoriented, anxious, and isolated. That we avoid at all cost.

Usually we are unaware of what we are doing to keep the system intact. Like people on a seesaw, when the weight changes on one side we instinctively do something to change the other side. Picture this: another mother and father are fighting and the seesaw threatens to get off balance. Mom is backing away from Dad and might leave altogether. Dad moves in closer to the center to hold onto her. That's the cue for one of the kids to hop on the seesaw, right in the middle, shifting his or her weight as needed to keep both parents in the game. This is a powerful position, more power than a child can easily handle. How does a child keep both parents in the game? Sometimes by getting into trouble; sometimes by developing a physical or emotional symptom. Having a bicycle accident. Failing math. Becoming unable to fall asleep at night.

In a study on family interaction, J. P. Spiegel found that when there were clearly complementary roles in a family, there was greater equilibrium. The couple who took turns drinking is a good illustration. They are obviously complementary, they balance each other, and chances are they will live out their lives together. In their system it does not matter who is drinking and who is sober. What is important is that one complement the other. There are endless balancing acts among couples. For example, in some couples, one partner is a saint and the other a sinner; one causes problems and the other soothes and pacifies; one is clean and healthy and the other likes dark, smoky dens. If one should change, the other might leave, or more likely, take over the partner's role. A woman told of ministering to her depressed man for ten years. When he finally decided to leave the family she took on all of the symptoms of his depression.

The role that one person plays does not "cause" the other's role. Rather, in the family system, our roles serve the function of keeping the others in their roles. Thus the wife's drinking serves to keep her husband dry. His being dry serves the function of keeping her drinking. When one partner is drinking, the interaction and contact between them is severely limited. With sobriety comes the possibility of genuine relationship and closeness, or of the opposite, genuine relationship and outright enmity. Either way, balance is upset and the anxiety level soars. The function of the drinking itself would seem to be to maintain a comfortable distance between the two so that the system will survive.

What may seem like random happenings in our families are generally the result of our efforts, unconscious though we may be of them, to keep the system operating. Like parts of the body that work with utmost urgency to keep the body alive, so members of the family do the best they can to maintain the family system. The parts—that is, the members—are working for the survival of the whole family system.

Healthy systems are those that meet the challenges of life, of growth and change, in ways that foster the well-being of all of the members. They change as needed. The members recognize the passage of time; they make new rules and drop outmoded interactions. When privacy is suddenly demanded by the eight-year-old, it is given. When lap-sitting and snuggling are no longer appropriate, it is not encouraged. Transition times in a family mean altering rules and creating new roles. When the first child goes off to pre-school, he or she does not come home the same baby; the interaction at home cannot continue as it was. In a healthy system nobody has to get sick or go crazy when the oldest child prepares to leave home, when the youngest becomes a teen, or when a new baby is born.

In families with considerable stress, the urgency to keep the system intact and in some kind of balance takes precedence over individual needs of growth and health. The child who remains in the parental bed for years is not moving to the next stage of development. The troublesome boy who spends all his time distracting his parents from their marital problems is not getting on with the business of growing up.

Attempts to keep the system together do not start out as full-blown craziness. They begin as behavior that in itself is harmless. A youngster does not want to go to school one day and is allowed to stay home. Mother stays home from work, too. Will this be a one-time occurrence or become a pattern? A child plays with her food at the table. Mother says, Eat up. Dad says, Leave her alone, maybe she's not feeling well. There is nothing evil about that scene; it is hardly out of the ordinary, repeated in countless households at one time or another. Yet troublesome behavior is ineffectual at taking hold *unless parents cooperate*. If the ground is fertile, however—that is, the action or interaction meets some implicit need of the parents—then it becomes the seed that is sown and takes root. It becomes Dad and daughter against Mom; daughter is on her way toward serious eating disorders and ruined health.

The innocent evil that is being perpetrated in these cases is the unintentional thwarting of the growth and independence of the child. It comes down to the survival of the system versus the development and growth toward autonomy of the youngster. What the system needs for survival always takes precedence.

A teenage girl comes home with her hair colored pink. Mother is amused. Father is horrified. Teenagers are noted for shocking their parents, one way or another. In this case, however, the ground is fertile. Mom and daughter form a coalition against Dad. The girl escalates her outrageous behavior. She puts a safety pin through her ear and sometimes doesn't come home at night. Mother becomes less and less amused. The girl becomes "the problem."

In another case a boy is caught shoplifting. In numerous families this is an isolated happening. In another family it signals the beginning of serious delinquency.

A mother feels depressed and takes a couple of glasses of wine before dinner. Does this woman need to balance her family system by taking on a serious symptom? Dad decides to invite his colleague, a young woman, out to lunch. A one-time thing or part of a critical balancing act in the system? What makes the difference? What are the conditions that encourage a family member to sacrifice health or well-being to keep everybody together?

For one thing, we frequently do not notice what is going on within our family. We are unaware of the shifts that could inform us that the family system is in trouble. Who says, "My, how you've grown!" or "You've really gotten gray"? Not the people who see us every day, but those who come into our lives after a long time. The gradual changes that take place in a family are like the slow shifting of sand from one area of the coast to another. We do not notice, until our beach is denuded. Suddenly we have a crisis; only rocks remain. Since some crises build gradually, we simply do not notice the trend. We do not go for check-ups. We remain ignorant, explaining away growing discomfort and inconvenience, until our lives are so disrupted we can no longer ignore the signs.

The ground becomes more fertile in anticipation of change. The oldest child reaches the teen years; there is no holding back his changing voice, her developing breasts. What behavior will follow these new developments? The youngest is soon to finish school and leave home. How will the parents make it with no kids to focus on? Shaky systems fear change. People become more rigid in their roles. This means everyone does what he or she has been doing, only more so. The angel becomes more angelic; the devil, more devilish. Mother's anger reaches unknown heights, Father is more distant than ever. Previously there was a comfortable complementarity that everyone could live with, but when family members become more polarized and more inflexible they reach a dangerous point. The more rigid the system, the less able it is to sail on in the stormy seas. Attempts to keep the system intact are the first order of business, but paradoxically the attempts at solutions create more serious problems. Each person retreats further and further into his or her role. There is less and less contact as each one feels more threatened. Violence, which may have been safely contained before, is more apt to erupt. The emotional or physical symptoms of the child increase in intensity and demand attention by an outsider—a doctor, a therapist, a law official. What began as a way to ease anxiety and keep the system together becomes the indecipherable problem that brings the family to crisis.

In one family when the mother had a breakdown, the father followed with his breakdown. The mother's sister succumbed and shortly after, her brother. The woman who told this had been twelve years old during this dreadful time, the oldest child in the family. She stopped talking for a few months. The chaos was too much. She carried on the only way she was able: she retreated.

As we have seen in previous chapters, children are frequently used to maintain equilibrium in the system. Sometimes it is difficult to tell whether they volunteer or are enlisted; probably some of each. Very young children are quick to respond to the increasing anxiety of an upset system, as in the case of the interrupting son with the bloody tooth, and with the quarreling sisters. They know precisely when to hop on the seesaw to balance the system. Whatever mechanism works becomes standard procedure, always with the cooperation of the other members of the family.

The family system that we grew up with is etched within each of us. We always remember the patterns of interaction that were repeated daily. Even those who say they do not remember anything of their childhood find that what is not in the conscious memory remains in the unconscious memory to be relived, over and over. The feelings, the actual physical reactions, facial expressions and tensing of muscles, the automatic responses— these are relics that exert strong influence long, long after our childhood years. We seem compelled to re-create the roles we took in our family in situation after situation with friends, lovers, marriage partners, and our children. In our present, we replicate what we knew in our past.

Being a part of our own system makes it difficult, but not impossible, to perceive what is going on in our family. If we tune to the right channel we can ferret out the rules and the roles that govern us. We can discern the repetitive patterns at our own dinner tables. Undoubtedly you have seen a photograph of yourself that revealed an unfamiliar aspect of you. "That doesn't look like me" was probably your reaction. Or perhaps you have heard a conversation that you took part in on tape that surprised you. You had not realized you were giggly, or overbearing, or faltering. Cameras and tapes are not necessary, but they are helpful. I remember one of our first home movies, "A Winter Walk on the Beach," which showed our family playing out a familiar interaction. The oldest son shoved one of his brothers toward the water, I got angry and shook my finger, scolding my oldest son, who was laughing. In how many versions of this theme did we all participate? How incapable I was, we all were, to change that interaction, although there was pain for everyone. I frequently felt like a victim of the system rather than one of the creators of the system.

What we need to do occasionally is to stop the action for a minute and take a look as if through a lens; to listen as if with a recorder; to get an outsider's view. We need only to step out of the system momentarily to perceive what our dance looks like. This in itself is a shift in the system, for when you step out of the system, when you stop dancing, for that second you are not part of the action. When you observe or talk about your system you are at another level. You are on another channel. From that vantage point you are in a position to make a new move, say a new line, respond in a way that is faithful to you rather than to your role in a faltering system. No matter how insignificant that first small step may seem, it is a step toward creating a change for the better in your system.

7 | Looking at Your System

How are we to find out the real story that we are living? There are no special X-rays to take pictures of family systems, no Cat-scans to examine how we function, no check-ups to detect signs of trouble. Our family mythology hoodwinks us. We miss what is right under our noses.

In *Family Therapy Techniques*, Salvador Minuchin describes what happens with a family of Mother, Father, and two-year-old son who are in his office. When the child, Frank, spills a box of chalk, Dr. Minuchin asks the parents to have Frank put the chalk back in the box. He watches and listens to the father and mother as they instruct the boy to do this. Each parent has a very different style. The father says, "Put the chalk in the box" and resumes his conversation with Minuchin. The mother gets up out of her chair and, standing near the box, says in a "firm but friendly" voice, "Frank, come here and put the chalk in the box." The boy does most of the task, but the mother has to call him back a couple of times. Each time the father, "in a peremptory voice," tells Frank to put the chalk back in the box, the mother gets the child to complete the task. When the parents are asked who is the competent person in controlling Frank, both "identify the father as the person who is competent in controlling Frank and the mother as soft and inefficient."

This is what family mythology does. It conceals the obvious. Anyone looking at a videotape of the scene in the office would have to agree that Mother was indeed competent. Minuchin asks the question "Since the mother is efficient and competent in the area of control, how is it that everyone in the family agrees that she is inefficient in this area?" He concludes that in order for there to be harmony in the functioning of the mother and father as the "parental subsystem," they must be seen, not as they really are, but she as "soft and inefficient" and he as "competent."

Healthy families are found to have a realistic view of what is going on in the family with a minimum of concealment and pretense. They see what is going on and call it as it really is. On the other hand, unhealthy families tend to create a fantasy about family members, about reasons for their behavior, their thoughts, and feelings. Mystification and mythology prevail. The family members reside in a world where things and people are not as they appear. There is little overlap between the family's "reality" and outside reality. An unbiased observer's view of such a family and their interaction would be significantly different from the story concocted by the family.

Difficult it may be, but until we cast a cold eye at the reality of who we are and what we are doing, unless we bring our parenting out of the cave of the unconscious, we will perpetuate the innocent evil in our own family. An important requirement for all of us who are concerned parents, then, is resolutely to look at, and see, what is actually going on in our families.

In view of our emotional entrapment in our families, the pervasive distortion of family mythology and individual self-image, is it possible for us to see and hear what our own family is doing? Probably not entirely; but without doubt more than we do.

We have no trouble perceiving what is non-threatening or neutral, what in no way jars us; however, we avoid upsetting our basic premises about how the world is and how people are. And whatever seems threatening or in some way damaging to our personal view of ourselves, or to the family system as we know it, will have a hard time breaking through the crust to our consciousness. If you believe that you treat all of your children the same way, that you show no favoritism, would you ever be able to see evidence to the contrary? The example from Minuchin shows us that what is threatening is not necessarily "bad." In fact, competency is generally considered good. Yet in the above situation Mother's competence was carefully screened out of everyone's awareness, for both her husband's protection and her own. You may, indeed, feel anxious at the thought of taking a look at what is, of uncovering what you have persistently screened out. A part of the mythology of almost every family is that we are so fragile, we need protection from experiencing what is.

If you are willing to elbow your way through the

mythology surrounding your own family interaction, here are a few reminders that may help. The first reminder is: we are all human and therefore less than "perfect." When we forget this fact, we are loath to get in touch with anything that would remind us. We relentlessly strive for some ideal "perfection" and we never achieve it. Our internalized "shoulds" are forever reminding us how we do not measure up; they make it hard for us to be ordinary people who forgive ourselves, our weaknesses and trespasses. No wonder we deny what we do, feel, and want, and instead substitute our mythology.

Remember that the others in the family are also human and are likely to fall short of some hypothetical standard of perfection. Looking at the family system is not an exercise in blaming yourself or another, nor is it about turning one person into a scapegoat: "This whole mess is your fault."

Our mythology often provides us with the illusion that we are living up to certain internalized "truths." For example, if a woman holds two "truths," first, that she should be a good wife, and second, a good wife should never be more competent than her husband, then she is not going to recognize her competence. Like the youngsters who deny their experience when it contradicts their parents' view of reality, we deny our experience if it contradicts a more important truth. Our more important truths, as parents, are frequently based on old shoulds, and they are generally vague, as in "I should be a good wife." Sometimes our truths are based on the maxims of our parents and become second-hand mythology, as in "A good wife should never be more competent than her husband."

123

Many of our truths are hidden in the recesses of the cellar of the house with the three levels referred to earlier. We can see the top level of interaction, and when we make the effort we can tune into the "systems level" below. But below that is an underlying level of "epistemological premises," those beliefs we took in without even being conscious of them. They wield the greatest power. "To love means to suffer." "People are bad to begin with and, left to themselves, will continue to be bad." "To be a parent is to be disappointed." Our dealings with one another are the outward manifestion of our deep-rooted presumptions. You will discover some of your basic premises that rule your interactions as you pay attention to the behavior patterns in your family. The questions that follow in this chapter will help.

Old shoulds and second-hand mythology cover much of life, thwarting our efforts to get in touch. To help tease out your old mythology, pay attention to what you say in your head. Listen to what you say to yourself about your own actions. "I should never get so upset." "I should be more patient." "I shouldn't let my kids get away with that." And listen to what you say to yourself about others' actions, since we direct our shoulds at others as well as at ourselves. "A wife shouldn't depend on her husband so much." "Children should always respect their parents." From that internal monologue you will uncover much old material that, like the bottom of a compost heap, needs to be turned over and exposed to the air and light. Only then does it become useful.

To use your discoveries in a productive way the first thing to do is simply acknowledge your find as an anthropologist discovers a lost article from an ancient culture. Look at it with interest, perhaps amusement, make a mental note of it, and notice how you use it in your life. Do not throw it away. You might create a "mental museum" for the artifacts and use them carefully, with awareness, with humor, if and when you want to. The second reminder, then, is to become gradually aware of, and set aside, your old shoulds and your stale mythology, long enough to allow for a whiff of fresh reality.

The fact is we are as we are and we do what we do in relation to our families. Our mythology may protect us from seeing and hearing, from facing up to ourselves and our family members, but it does not change what we do or how we are; nor does it protect our children. Ironically, it is our pretensions about how we are and what we are doing that are the most damaging, living in a crippling dream world and keeping us out of touch with ourselves and each other.

One of the shoulds that we have all learned is that we should correct wrongs, especially those we ourselves commit. What a muddle we create then. If we open our eyes and see what part we are playing in our family system, we immediately think: "I should do something different. But I don't know how to be different." What activates greater anxiety than the risk of stepping out of a familiar role into new experience? "If I do something different, what will happen? 'They' won't love me, everything will fall apart, I'll be all alone, I'll die."

The third reminder, then, is: adopt the attitude that you need not remodel yourself and the others, nor revolutionize your family system before tomorrow morning. This way you will see and hear and experience a great deal more, and you will not be immobilized by the inevitable and endless conflict: I should/I can't; I should/I can't.

If you feel the urge come over you to do something when the workings of the family system begin to come into focus for you, use your head—not to beat against the wall of well-instituted patterns you have all built up over time, but to realize that you see an outmoded solution in action. Hold the blame and the inclination to "educate" everybody. Become aware of any excuses you make for yourself or any of the others concerning family interaction. Experience your part, whether it is an active or passive role. Remember that each of you contributes to the total picture. In very small ways you may gradually do something different. You may comment on what you are doing, for example. You may withdraw your support, your part in whatever destructive or unpleasant pattern you may discover.

We use many screens to obscure reality and hold onto our mythology. Our judgments are one such screen. One mother asked me, "Is it really possible to look at members of your family without making judgments?" Apparently, for her it was not. Each interaction she had with her children and husband was an exercise in influencing them in such a way that she would seem not to be trying to influence them! She confessed that for her to simply see and hear her children and husband she would have to imagine that she was not connected to them.

This woman pretends that she is not trying to influence the others. Why does she have to pretend? Who is she fooling? Not her children or her husband. They feel constantly manipulated and controlled by her although they never talk openly to her about it. Like a young child who thinks others cannot see him because he has his hands in front of his eyes, she hides this controlling woman from herself and imagines the others will never notice she is there. She has a strong judgment against being that kind of wife and mother. Her mother was like that.

At each encounter she makes judgments about how the other members of her family should be and what they should do. By her attitude and actions she shows that she does not trust any of them to have one ounce of sense. Yet this is not, as one might suspect, a family of idiots. Her husband is a professional man who earns a good living and her three children are all perfectly bright kids. In her rational mind she knows they are capable. Yet her ever-present judgment about each one is "This person is not trustworthy to be, act, feel, in the way that I think would be best for him or her." With all the judgments about what kind of wife and mother she should be, plus those about how her husband and children should be, there is little chance she can push her way through to some realistic view of the family patterns—unless a crisis threatens.

The fourth reminder: become aware of and drop your judgments. If you are not conscious of them, you can track down your judgments by noticing the adjectives you use to describe the various members of the family. Notice, also, your reactions when you approach your partner or your children, your tone of voice, whether you expect an argument, whether you feel defensive. The more you are aware of your reactions, the easier will be the experience of getting in touch, the more judgments will become explicit.

Another screen that dovetails right in with the judgments screen is expectations. With our expectations we superimpose who we think is there, who we would like to be there, or who we fear is there on the actual people we are dealing with. If your daughter was expected to be a son, and you expected him to be your buddy, go to your school, and perpetuate your business and your name, chances are your disappointment will come between you and this child. "Worst fear" type of expectations especially block out reality. Those are the most insidious. Think of the boy whose mother was certain he would be retarded. He was completely hidden behind the screen of her worst fear. She interacted with him *as if* he were retarded rather than with him as he actually was: a perfectly bright, normal child.

We all have expectations for our kids. Some we are aware of. Others, not. One young mother tells of her feelings of disappointment when she was told that her daughter was not perfectly healthy at birth. Of course she expected a perfect baby. "If she's not perfect I don't want her" was her initial reaction, for which she found it hard to forgive herself. What kind of mother would not want her child? A bad one obviously. The imperfection in the child was corrected and the mother soon came to accept and love her baby. The child had not lived up to her mother's expectation that she would be perfect; therefore she was unacceptable. Dudley Moore, the actor, tells in an interview that his mother once told him that when, at his birth, she found out that he had a clubfoot she wanted to kill him.

Our expectations for our children keep us in a constant state of discontent making comparisons between them and what we expected—some arbitrary standard of behavior or development, some "ideal" or "normal" child who never existed. For a real child to try to fill the shoes of a figment of our imagination or memory, a creature of fiction or of dreams, is an impossible task. Our expectations, whether they are positive or negative, lie like a heavy blanket on our children and hide them from our view. Their self-esteem languishes under the weight. To help become aware of your expectations and how they interfere with contact with your child, notice when you feel disappointed or discontented, when you are comparing your son or daughter to "Johnny next door," or "your cousin Betty," or "when I was your age."

Our negative expectations do their own brand of damage. "He'll come to no good." "She's going to turn out to be another Aunt Marie." Such pessimistic predictions, as they are repeated over the months and years, become self-fulfilling prophecies, forebodings for the future, for ourselves or our children, warping their lives as well as our own. The mother of a friend of mine expected not to be loved. She would stroke the dog in front of her children saying, "You're the only one who loves me." Frequently she lamented, "Only the dog loves me." The children were baffled. They thought they loved her. They never knew what more they were supposed to be, or do. They came to dislike their mother for never recognizing them and their acts of love toward her, for making them failures as loving children. This mother, as you may suspect, had grown up with a mother who did not love her.

It is more satisfying to stay in the present and forget about catastrophic predictions. Your real children are right there, needing you to forget your expectations and see, hear, and respond to them, to appreciate them and interact with them for who they are.

With those five reminders—first, we are all ordinary people with normal frailties, weaknesses, and fears; second, old shoulds may blind us to our behavior, our feelings, and our desires; third, telling ourselves that we must do something about what we see and hear will keep us from seeing and hearing in the first place; fourth, judgments keep us out of touch; and fifth, expectations may keep us from responding to the reality of a child, especially those expectations of which we are unaware—getting in touch becomes a real possibility. Your eye will become trained and your ear sharper, and you will better be able to experience yourself in your interactions.

Here are important areas to look at to help you become acquainted with your family system. When you read the following questions some answers may pop into your head. This is unavoidable. However, these answers may be connected either to reality or to mythology. Put those answers aside and practice discovering the answers principally through your eyes and ears, and especially through your experience over a period of time with your family.

Who has the power in your family? In the book *No Single Thread: Psychological Health in Family Systems*, Jerry Lewis and his co-authors report that in those families which are considered healthy, the parents are in charge. Mother and Father, the "parental subsystem," make the rules, decide what behavior is acceptable, support each other, and set the tone for the interaction between parents and children, and between the children. How is power used? Is it used benevolently? Or is it an oppressive power, demanding rigid conformity? Is there mutual support between family members or are there victims? If there has been a divorce, how do the parents share the power now? These questions can help to acquaint you with the issue of power in your family.

In the area of power, family mythology may cloud reality. Paradoxical power arrangements are common. An alcoholic father may seem to be in control, since his wife and children are afraid of him. However, his wife may have taken over as the real head of the household, making decisions, earning money, and running the show. In that case, who is really in control? For another example, consider the mother who needs to be needed to such an extent that she keeps a child infantile. It appears that the mother is in control; at the same time, however, the child remains helpless, demanding, and totally dependent on her. This continues into adulthood. Somewhere along the line the mother has lost control and the result is a kind of mutual victimization.

In some cases, members of a family who feel without power get chronically sick. Having symptoms gives power: power to get special attention, to get one's own way, to curtail the activities of the others.

We think of power as power over somebody else to get what we want, and in families it is often used like that. How do people get what they need and want in your family? Does each one use the same method? Who has the loudest voice? Who has the quickest temper? Some people get what they want by being good, others by being the squeaky wheel. How does Mother get what she wants? And Dad? Power and influence go together. How do the older children influence a younger brother or sister to cooperate in a scheme? Maybe they use affection, or shame, or threats such as, "I won't like you anymore," or "I won't give you any ice cream," or "Do I have to hit you?" Or maybe they use irrefutable logic and clever persuasion. We parents do well to listen to our children. They often serve as an echo giving us the reality, not the mythology, of how we use or abuse our power.

Power is also expressed in taking care of, comforting, and supporting others, so keep that in mind as you look for who has power and how they use it. This is an important point when considering the special child in the family and the position he or she occupies. The special child is the one who is blamed as "the problem," perhaps made the scapegoat, and, in the eyes of an outside helper, is in need of rescuing. Yet the special child, in some way, experiences that he or she is taking care of the family, is making the system work. There is power in that position, and the child is reluctant to be released. One of the brilliant twists that some family therapists have used productively is to suggest other ways for the problem child to save the family, ways that won't be detrimental to his or her development.

Sometimes family members form alliances. Perhaps two children stick together to increase their influence over other children or over the parents. In some families one parent and a child form a coalition against the other parent and other children. Look at the interaction in your family with this in mind. Who is aligned with whom? Look for the two who always agree, who stick up for each other, who speak for and support one another. A power alliance between one of the parents and a child is a distortion in the family power structure and will take its toll on the child who is used in this way.

Grandparents may play a role in this kind of team. A

parent can keep his or her mother as co-captain or even general. And a grandparent and grandchild against one of the parents makes a powerful combination. An out-of-control child—and this could be a four-year-old who has frequent tantrums or a twenty-one-year-old who cannot leave home, will not get a job, and makes life miserable for the family—is undoubtedly encouraged in this behavior by at least one parent. The alliance may not be explicit; the parent who is lending support may be doing so unaware of his or her part in the plot.

If you discover such a coalition in your family system, cast your eye on the relationship between the parents. If the coalition is made up of Father and child, is this the only way Father can wield any power? Does he use the child to fight his battles with Mother? If Mother has taken one of the children as a special ally, where is Father? Is this Mother's way of keeping Father out? Coalitions are a "solution" that begin as an effort to keep the family system from self-destructing and are perpetuated by everyone in the system, with potentially serious consequences for the child involved.

How are feelings handled in your family? Which feelings are acceptable? Which feelings are expressed and acted out? Which are repressed? Is it the same for each family member, or are there different rules for different people? Bob Jr. told me that as a grown man he was home for the holidays with his family and dared to disagree with his father. "We don't have disagreements," said Bob Sr. "That makes me angry," answered Bob Jr. "We don't get angry" was the reply. Is it safe to get angry in your family? In the case of Bob Sr., it had not been safe. When his mother and father had gotten angry at each other they had terrified him, chasing each other around with hatchets. It follows that he, Bob Sr., instituted the rule "No anger" for his family.

In your family, are children taught what is "proper" to feel? Do feelings have to be justified or "make sense"? Is it possible to have a good cry for no apparent reason? Are there "right" feelings to have and "wrong" feelings? For example, a five-year-old who bursts into tears when Father comes home after a long trip is told, "You should be happy. You shouldn't cry."

A four-year-old girl was instructed to throw flowers on the lowered coffin at her grandmother's funeral. She was a very serious, controlled child, who had been enlisted to comfort her bedridden grandmother during the last weeks before her death. The child's feelings of fright and confusion, added to her nervousness at performing her task to perfection, completely eclipsed any grief she might have felt. To the horror of all the grown-ups gathered there, and to her own horror as well, she laughed at the crucial moment. The wrong feelings! The wrong expression! How could she laugh when she had loved her grandmother so much and felt so sad at her death? Her scandalized parents chastised her in front of everyone. The impact of that devastating experience stayed with her for years. At last, in her fifties, she talked about this experience for the first time and confessed that every time she heard of the death of someone she knew she had an uncontrollable urge to laugh. She attended funerals only when she could not avoid it, and struggled each time to keep her laughter contained.

As children, many of us learned that our feelings were not important and should be denied; any expression had to be hidden. So much confusion results when feelings are evaluated, some accepted as healthy, others as bad or dangerous. Feelings and emotions in and of themselves are neither good nor bad. They just are. They are a part of being alive and stem from actual reactions in our bodies. The importance of feelings cannot be overemphasized. "To know who one is, an individual must be aware of what he feels," says Alexander Lowen in *Betrayal of the Body*. Without our feelings to inform us of how we are, we lose touch and substitute how we think we are. We gradually become alienated from our bodies, from ourselves.

The young child lumps together feeling and acting; there is no separation between the two. Actions are the natural and simultaneous expressions of feelings. A child feeling uneasy or tense wiggles and squirms, or perhaps acts shy. A parent criticizes, "Stop that. Don't be like that." Or the child strikes out and breaks something. The parent comes down hard. Crying, hitting, and biting are intrinsic forms of self-expression. When we criticize and put a stop to such actions (which, of course, is part of the socializing process) children get the messages "Don't feel that" as well as "Don't do that." They learn that their feelings as well as their actions are unacceptable. They need to learn, instead, that having feelings is desirable; acting on them is not always so. The parents' manner toward the child communicates an attitude of acceptance or rejection. The words "I understand how you feel but . . ." are ineffective when feigned. Notice whether members of your family look to one another for permission to be angry, or scared, or sad. This is an indication that they don't trust that their reactions to what is happening around them are acceptable. Who is the authority on what is acceptable?

Anger, rage, grief, and hate—were you taught these were bad when you were a child? Can you tolerate them in your children? Do you have acceptable ways to express feelings in your house? Do you have ways to convey that feelings are healthy, even when some self-expression must be modified or sublimated or postponed? We are all capable of a broad range of feelings of every intensity. Who in your family has the most intense feelings? Who is considered "the sensitive one"? Who can be boisterous? Is there a point when people in the family "feel too much"? In one family a daughter was more excitable than the rest of the family members. To calm her down one of the parents doused her with cold water. How is too much excitement handled in your family?

What is the general emotional climate? Cold and suppressive? Warm and affectionate? Do people touch each other? Who does not get touched? What is the parents' basic view of mankind? Are we born evil, driven by base appetites and desires, needing to be controlled in order to be good, needing to have the "devil" beaten out of us? Or are we born good, needing firm guidance, love, and encouragement to develop all of our potential?

What do you do about differences in your family? Is individuality allowed, or is there one "right" way to be? One of the most obvious differences is sex. Can girls express their "girlness" and boys their "boyness"? Can a girl do "boy" things and a boy do "girl" things? Is there an attempt to blur the difference? Another obvious difference is age. Are age differences ignored or are there diverse expectations, privileges, and responsibilities that apply to different members? Are various tastes in food, clothing, activities frowned on? Can Democrats and Republicans live side by side?

Must family members conform to certain imposed standards of behavior to be acceptable? Are these standards clear? Are they the same for everyone? Are there requirements for being loved? Are they the same for everyone? Does "being fair" mean that everyone is treated the same, regardless of whether it is appropriate to their age and development? To carry "fairness" to extremes can result in unfairness; for example, to spend the same amount for gifts for each child, regardless of his or her interests and age.

In well-functioning families individuality is respected. These families allow for variety. In such families are found "unique, impressive, individual characteristics," not just "bland, plain vanilla," as expressed by Lewis et al. in their book on healthy family systems. What is the prevailing attitude in your family? Is it "I'm O.K.—you're O.K., even if you are different from me"? Or "You're not O.K. if you are different and you will be put down for it"? Do people accept each other as individuals, with private and personal thoughts, experiences, and dreams? Is each member encouraged to develop his or her self, to be and become, to march, at least part of the time, to his or her own drummer?

Are conflicts overt or covert? Can you and others in the family express different opinions? Are you asking for a fight if you do? How do you handle complaints? Do people argue in your family? Notice which members get into conflicts and what the subject matter is. Are the conflicts chronic? That is, do they go on and on with no resolution? When two people have a conflict, does a third person get in on it? Who is the family peace-maker?

Do you handle conflicts rationally? Is negotiation used? Is physical force used? What are the rules governing this? When "nothing else works" do you use a forceful approach? Would you call it "mild punishment" or does the force get "abusive"? Slapping and spanking children are generally accepted in America as "necessary, normal, and good," according to Murray A. Straus, Richard J. Gelles, and Suzanne K. Steinmetz, the authors of *Behind Closed Doors: Violence in the American Family*. Do you agree with this?

The California Task Force on Positive Parenting reported vast increases in all forms of family violence during the 1970's: homicide, child abuse, sexual abuse, and juvenile suicide. According to Michael Gordon, executive director of Californians Preventing Violence, that trend continues in the 1980's. Does anyone get violent in your family? Feelings of powerlessness and frustration frequently increase the chance of violent acting out. The father who has lost his job, for example, is more apt to be violent at home. Straus and his co-authors list eighteen occurrences that produce stress within families, among them trouble at work, death of someone close, serious health problems, separation or divorce, a child kicked out of school. They suggest that there is a connection between stress and violence, that "stress does increase the chances that a family will resort to abusive violence."

How is force, if it is used, justified? "Spare the rod and spoil the child." "It didn't hurt me and my father beat me regularly." "You made me do it." "You asked for it." Is the perpetrator of violence turned into the

138

victim? "This hurts me more than it does you." Is force justified by righteousness? "We must transform this fallen creature into an acceptable, rational, human being." "This is a question of good against evil." The battle of good versus evil has led to the most severe forms of abuse, to uncontrollable wrath against the child who has provoked the parent.

If you have the feeling that you have been bombarded by all of these questions, relax and take a deep breath. The questions in this chapter are meant to provide direction for you as you begin the formidable and essential task of discovering the patterns of interaction in your family, interaction of which you yourself are a part. Each question is a light pointing to a place to look, a way to listen, a moment to experience and react. It is possible for all of us to see and hear more of what we are doing in our family system. Simply the process of reading through the questions may have excited your curiosity and sharpened your perception. The next step is to talk together about what you see, hear, and experience: to communicate.

8 | Communication and Changing the Family System

One of the most common complaints that therapists hear is, "We can't communicate." Couples can't talk to each other. Frustrated parents can't get through to their children. Children complain that parents never listen.

For families it is especially important to know what is going on with one another. Otherwise we only guess. We interact with mystery people, and too often we miss connections. When we know what makes someone tick, we get interested. We care.

We learn what is going on with one another through our communication. In large part, we create ourselves, each other, our relationships, and our systems by our interaction. Who we are, our relationships, and our family system are all inextricably woven into our communication.

The names we call each other define our relationships. Mother, Father, Child, Boy, Girl, and such remind us of our place in the family. A young couple I know took to addressing each other as Husband and Wife during the first weeks of their marriage: "Husband, where are you?" "I'm here, Wife," as if to remind themselves of their new relationship. Kid Brother and Kid Sister are effective reminders: "I was here before you were. A little respect, please."

Listen to the communication in your house and you will find out about the covert rules of how people relate to one another. Who talks to whom? Who initiates conversations? Who asks questions? Who puts whom down? With these four questions in mind, the relationships in the family will gain clarity. Who is "low man" on the totem pole? Who is at the top? How is this manifested in the interaction? For example, when a child interrupts a parent and apologizes for doing so, the relationship between parent and child, at that moment, is defined: the child is subordinate. The parent who interrupts the child without an apology similarly defines the relationship. When Father asks daughter, "Did you clean your room today?" and Mother gives an excuse why daughter did not clean her room, the relationships between Mother and daughter, Mother and Father, Father and daughter are all being created and defined, *but only for that moment*. The curious thing about families is that their interaction becomes repetitive and predictable. The identical patterns appear again and again, day after day, keeping the relationships and the system exactly as they have been.

Each interchange says something about the relationship of the people talking. Do messages go directly from person to person or is there someone who relays messages? A woman told me that years after she was married and had moved to another state her father would call her from the garage of his house and ask her to call her mother, who was in the kitchen, and tell her to bring him a cup of coffee.

No matter how you look at it communication is complex and constant. Just the way we sit in silence communicates something to those around us. Each gesture, the way you hold your head or draw a breath, all behavior, except in isolation, is communication. So when people say they cannot communicate they are talking about a special kind of communication. They are talking about being seen, being heard, and being acknowledged. They are talking about making contact, about having an impact on one another.

What you talk about in your family and how you do your talking sculpts the individuals and the interaction between them. It determines whether you get in touch with each other or not. Let us look at and listen to the family at the dinner table from Chapter 6. Mother sits down at the table and says, "Let's have no bickering at the table tonight," whereupon the bickering starts. Mother does not make it all happen single-handedly; she only plays her role. The result is a total family creation. She is joined on cue by each of the children in his role: Child #1, "It's always Johnny who starts it." Child #2, punctuating with an elbow in the ribs of his brother, "Shut up, I do not." Father plays his role by staying out of the action until Mother calls on him: "Please do something." This family, in their everyday behavior, through their patterns of communication, are creating their system, re-creating it over and over in the same mold. With their communication they generate exactly what they have. It never "just happens."

The family scene above is a re-creation of the family dance—the covert, unconscious ritual that is predictable, and "feels right" to everybody. They do not necessarily find it pleasant or enjoy the interaction. Each member comes in on cue, each one plays his or her role in the way that is expected by the other members. It is familiar and comfortable. It defines clearly each person's part in the family system. Who or what is making them do it, not just once, but repeatedly? Is it simply a habit? Surely that is a part of the answer—the habit of automatic family interaction, of no real contact: who sees? who hears? who responds? The roles are clear but the family members have no significance beyond the parts they play in this abortive family drama.

Preposterous as it may seem, let us suppose this game provides the players with precisely what they want. This means Mother wants the children to bicker. How might she profit from this interaction? For one thing, at least something is going on, an interaction that reassures her the connection between them is still there. What else? A chance to suffer with these boys who are too much for her. She is tired after a whole day of work, and now this. In addition, she assumes her "mother" role with her immediate family, pretending to be in charge, pretending to state her wishes, inducing a play in which she wins—by losing. She reinforces everything she "knows" about herself.

If Mother were to become aware that she wants the boys to bicker, that she has, in fact, been encouraging them, could she do with intention what she has been doing unconsciously? As she sits down to serve dinner, what would happen if she were to gently rub her hands together and with a smile on her face invite her boys: "O.K. kids, go to it." Would that work? Would they bicker? More likely she would succeed in putting a stop to the bickering. With that approach she would change the rules. No pretense, no role playing. She would send a clear message, simply saying what she wants. A change of rules brings about a change in interaction. It appears that she has a never-fail approach, possibly the one sure method to continue the family interaction as it is, to get apparently just what she wants, and take no responsibility for what she is doing. Without consciousness there is no self-responsibility.

But let us not single out Mother to blame. Child #1 profits and knows just how to run with the ball: he gains the role of the good guy. He gets to stay at the table with his folks. Child #2 profits: the role of the bad guy is his inheritance. He is the only one to whom Father talks or pays attention. Father gets what he wants. He is silent, withdrawn, until he is needed by Mother to keep order; he assumes the important "father" role.

All safe. All familiar. The system limps along full of pretense. Mother pretends she does not want the boys to bicker and that she cannot manage. One boy pretends to be good. One pretends to be bad. Father pretends to be in charge. The scene is set for Mother's double message. The explicit, "Don't bicker," is overshadowed by the implicit, "Go ahead, kids, bicker." So they do. *The implicit demand is always the stronger. They all get what they want but no one enjoys any triumph. There is no satisfaction.* By being tied to a rigid role in an unchanging script their communication is no longer a vehicle to express themselves, to connect spontaneously and energetically with themselves and each other.

Now let us assume that Mom and Dad care about each other and this family functions pretty well. Mother really wants to stop the nightly bickering at the table. She might go to Dad before dinner and say something like this: "I'm fed up with the bickering at dinner every night and Johnny's getting sent away from the table. I don't know what to do. Sometimes I feel so inept as a mother, which I know is crazy since I am so capable outside the house. Do you have any ideas about what we could do? I want to do something different."

Or maybe Dad goes to Mom and says, "Dinner's a hassle every night. Let's see if we can take over the conversation tonight—you and I talk like we used to before the kids were born. We used to talk in complete sentences, didn't we?"

In either case they step out of the old roles; they communicate person to person. Neither manipulates for hidden gains. Neither blames. Each one knows, "This is what I want." No pretense. They acknowledge that they are part of a couple, each needing something from the other. Both are saying, "We need to strengthen the parental sub-system." Of course couples do not think in those terms or use those words, yet simply by talking about the problem together they are doing just what needs to be done. They come together and take a position; they reclaim their partnership in parenting. This couple is setting a new scene calling for new scripts. They come to the table. Father smiles at Mother. They start to talk. Kids don't miss anything. The interaction must and will be different.

If the boys are tightly entrenched in their roles they

may fight to hold on. As one child said during a family therapy session, "I don't like it when things change in my family." They will interrupt, become more boisterous, escalate their behavior in any way they know how until Mother says to Dad, "Please put a stop to this." If Dad tells Johnny to leave the table they have succeeded in bringing everything back to "normal." The parents will have failed this time. They all slip back into the familiar. If this were to occur, Mom and Dad would have to be persistent. Two parents in agreement are an unbeatable team. Further attempts are called for, some encouragement for the boys to express themselves directly, some authentic responses to set the example of risking, of relinquishing the safe but empty role. As the Russian proverb states, "Man is not a mushroom; he does not grow in a day."

The one way of relating that is familiar is unfortunately easier than the hundred ways that are different. You do not have to pay any attention to the familiar. No change in consciousness is required. You expend a minimum of energy. There is little contact, little risk. You may not feel satisfied, but you can hang on safely to what you have.

If the family member who is hanging on the most tightly is one of the parents, then changes in the system come slowly, if at all. Suppose that Mother or Father alone attempts to alter the interaction at the dinner table by going to one or both of the boys with a plan and asking for cooperation. Temporary adjustments are possible; but lasting changes in the system are out of the question until the parents both support it. Otherwise, by whatever means possible, Mother or Father will sabotage changes. Alexander Lowen in *The Betrayal of the*

Body states simply, "All role playing involves mutual support and exploitation." Getting out of rigid role playing also involves mutual support and relinquishing exploitation of one another.

If the family has become severely dysfunctional, an outside person may be the one to call it like it is and introduce some changes in the system. Johnny might have gotten the idea that he must be out of the picture for the rest of the family to function. If he has sensed that the system is very tenuous, then leaving the table may not be enough. He might go to an extreme: delinquency, illness, suicide, or a fatal accident. He would not only remove himself, but, in this way, he would call for help as well. He has learned the family rule that everything is pretense: you say one thing when you mean something else, you do one thing when you want to do another. He has not learned that a clear call for help is very easy: you cry, "*Help*."

His destructive action would be an indirect cry to bring an outside person to the family scene, be it a law officer, social worker, doctor, or clergyman. Perhaps concerned friends, neighbors, or relatives would lend assistance. As a result of interventions by the outsider, the family might rally behind change. Johnny's call for help would have served its purpose. With mutual encouragement and support they could begin to talk, listen, and get acquainted. A healthier system would become a possibility, maybe a reality for them.

Your family may not be a bickering family. In whatever way your gang is communicating, so are you creating your system, and establishing and defining relationships. No one person's behavior is accidental or disconnected. You all have your history; you are each a part of the whole. As you listen to the communication in your family, keep this in mind: a single isolated statement is meaningless. Only when the statement is considered as relational, a piece of interaction, does it make any sense. Only in the context of who says it, to whom, in what tone of voice, when, what came before, and what comes after, do you have the necessary pieces of the puzzle that comprise the family system. Then, too, you may discover whether people are seen, heard, and responded to, not as roles, but as people.

A scene that took place in our kitchen some years ago will illustrate the difference. I have long since forgotten the content of the interchange between one of my sons and me, but I remember I was deep in the role of angry mother, shaking my finger at him, talking at him, when suddenly he dared to extricate himself from the role of bad boy, reached over and looked directly at me, and with apparent patience and affection ruffled the hair on my head. A surprise rush of tears was my response.

Family communication is full of ambiguities and confusion, usually stemming from our attempts to protect ourselves and others. This all-too-true-to-life example is taken from Anne Tyler's novel *Dinner at the Homesick Restaurant*. Cody, the ninth-grade son,

> had to keep things separate—his friends in one half of his life and his family in the other half. His mother hated for Cody to mix with outsiders. "Why don't you have someone over?" she would ask, but she didn't deceive him for a moment. He'd say, "Nah, I don't need anybody," and she would look pleased. "I guess your family is enough for you,

isn't it?" she would ask. "Aren't we lucky to have each other?"

Mother is torn between playing the role of the mother she thinks she ought to be, and being the lonely, frightened woman she is. Cody is a typical child in that he protects his mother. He deceives her as she deceives him. Neither one discloses what is really going on. They have long since become alienated from themselves and from each other.

Is your family dinner table like a poker table, where people win only by bluffing? Are statements of disclosure taken at face value or are people forever "trying to read between the lines?" Do others assume that the speaker is consciously or unconsciously deluding himself and others?

In your family do people express themselves? For example, "This is how I feel," or "This is what I want," or "This is what I don't like." Notice whether these kinds of statements are encouraged or discouraged. A common discouragement: "Why do you feel like that?" Then when a reason is stated, "That's not a good reason." "You shouldn't feel like that." "You always feel like that." "Don't be so sensitive." "Who asked you?" "We can't always have what we want." "You don't mean that." "You're just feeling like that because you're upset." Self-expression is easily quenched. Simply by drawing in a breath or letting out a breath, or by the way you put a question, you can upset the fragility of the moment. A mother asks her daughter, "We don't have any trouble understanding each other, do we?" The child says, after a moment, "No." Mother expels her breath and breaks into a pleased smile. Parents and spouses use such dampers, especially when they are fearful of hearing how the other feels.

The idea that we have to *do* something about how the other person feels keeps us from simply being a good listener. We jump out of the present and into some future time: "I must make this person feel O.K." Next rushes in the thought, "I can't do anything." Or, "I don't know what to do." Then we respond—not to the person who is talking, but out of our feelings of inadequacy, out of fear that we won't be able to fill the bill. I mentioned earlier my daughter's comment to me, "You ask me how I feel and when I tell you, you get mad at me." To be clear at a time like that is simply to say that you feel threatened or unsure of what to say or do.

Basically what we all want from those close to us is for them to really listen, openly, with contact, without all the extraneous judgments and evaluations, quick solutions and reassurances. You affirm someone's existence when you are present, when you listen and take that person seriously. To have our existence validated is vital at every age. Here is an example from the doctoral dissertation of Madeleine Wyrich on the subject of meta-communication and marriage.

> Valerie is very low and depressed. Chris, her husband, asks, "Tell me what is going on, why are you so depressed?" He continues in a caring and empathetic tone, "I can understand the thing with D. is bothering you, but I have the feeling it is more than that."
>
> Valerie responds after a short pause, in a very grave and hopeless voice, "I have no future."

>   Chris responds, "You have no future, well, that's
> a very serious thing."

This is quality communication; it includes three vital elements. First, Chris is willing to listen to his wife's feelings without taking upon himself to change her or the situation. Second, he takes seriously her experience in that moment, whether or not he understands, or agrees, or likes how she feels. Third, he responds in such a way that she feels valued by him.

The words we speak are only a minor part of what we communicate. "It's not what you say, it's how you say it." The emotional element, conveyed in the nonverbal aspects, packs the wallop. "I'm so happy to be with you," said with a flat voice, eyes looking away, and face expressionless, is not convincing. "I hate being with you," said with a delighted smile and a warm squeeze of the hand, gives a clear message to the listener, despite the apparent contradiction. Underneath many of the problems in family communication are the questions "How much do I want you to know about me?" and "How much do I want to know about you?" The less deception, the clearer the communication and the more the contact between people. The bickering family mentioned above had much deception and little contact.

There are times we unintentionally say one thing and mean another. There are times we do not know exactly what we do mean. We are complicated beings, often with mixed feelings and intentions. Frank Oz, who developed the character Yoda in the film *The Empire Strikes Back*, has said, "My job is to make a character come to life, making him varied, contradictory, and complex on several different levels." Yoda was an unforgettable character who indeed came to life for the viewers. We, like Yoda, are varied, contradictory, and complex whether we like to think of ourselves this way or not. Otherwise we are dull and two-dimensional, cardboard figures. Our complexity may make us interesting; it also makes us confusing to those around us, and sometimes to ourselves.

Lewis Carroll's famous Alice says, "I can't explain myself, I'm afraid, sir, because I am not myself, you see." We all have an "I" and "myself." A young woman said to me, "I spend a lot of time being fed up with myself." William James referred to "the hell we make for ourselves." This "I" and "myself" split starts early, when we disown those aspects of ourselves our parents did not like. We identify most often with those feelings and that behavior that our parents found acceptable and lovable. That's the "I." The "myself" is frequently thought of as the bad young kid, the part our parents did not want and we try to deny: the "not me." They are both parts of us and both demand expression. Thus I do things "in spite of myself," although "my head tells me I shouldn't," and I "listen to my heart."

These expressions remind us of our internal entanglements and confusions. Our words and our music may arise from different levels of our being. The mood you set with your voice may contradict the meaning of your words. Your facial expression may say, "This is just a joke," while your words are deadly serious. The non-verbal emotional undertone of communication is often sent and received at an unconscious level. It carries a persuasive truth about the sender, and the relationship between the speaker and the listener. Adults may choose to discount all but the verbal message when it suits their purpose ("But he said he loved me!") yet children, whose lives depend on knowing what is going on around them, especially the relationships that closely affect them, are intently observant and responsive to the nonverbal cues, the messages that do not lie.

We have discussed the double bind and how deleterious is its effect on youngsters who live with a constant dose of contradictory verbal and nonverbal messages. A Dutch psychiatrist, J. H. Van den Berg, writes in his book *Dubious Maternal Affection* of the damage done by a parent's attempts to cover his or her ambiguity toward the child by "acting like a good parent." He wrote, "A child can stand an underdose of real love more easily than an overdose of false love." The uncertainty created for the child is such that "he cannot move; cannot stir: he cannot develop his personality."

The whole business of "giving affection" is suspect to Van den Berg, who suggests that children need affection only because of the parents' ambivalence. As a parent it does not sit well when someone suggests that my show of affection toward my children may have been (maybe still is) harmful to them. However, "showing affection" is a far different experience from "being an affectionate parent." As affectionate parents our messages carry the underlying attitude of seeing, hearing, and validating the existence of our children. The danger, indeed the evil, comes into the picture when we parents are unaware of how we use our children for our emotional needs. Then our "false love," as Van den Berg calls it, or in the words of Christopher Lasch in *The Culture of Narcissism*, an "access of seemingly solicitous care but with little real warmth," is used for our own purposes: to increase our child's dependence, to give the parent a "love object," to play the child against the other parent, to impress the world, to assuage our own conscience, or whatever. Pretense poisons communication; it tends to infect whole families. Straight talk begets straight talk.

Parents set the tone for communication in the family. Listen to the members of your household. Are they clear? Notice whether they qualify, contradict, confuse, and distract one another. Be aware whether one person tries to convince the other of something. Observe whether they appear to listen to one another.

The listener, too, can make mincemeat of a message in many ways. An unwilling listener who deflects what you say, takes only a little piece of your message to throw back at you, or distorts your meaning does not engage in communication. That person is not interested in contact but rather in distance. Good listening entails letting the whole message in. Some people never hear anything good about themselves; any compliment sent their way is blocked. Only statements that make them feel bad and wrong get through. If bad and wrong messages are not coming their way, they twist things around so they hear what they want to hear. Others have a hard time hearing anything negative, hearing resentments, hearing anger. In some families there is a rule that no emotions can come through at all. "When you can speak in a calm voice, then you can come out of your room."

Parents and children become accomplished screeners; they do not hear what they do not want to hear. One mother was unusually straightforward in her blocking. When her twenty-year-old son came home from college and told her he was gay, she put her hands over her ears and said, "I didn't hear that. You never said that."

So much talk in families seems an attempt to mold and control that our ears become acutely sharp, maybe oversharp, in picking out and reacting to demands. Sometimes these demands are not there at all. Sometimes they are. "I hate newspapers all over the floor" is a statement about me. You hear, "Pick up the newspapers," or, "Get those kids of yours to pick up the newspapers." An important distinction exists between a statement of how I am or what I like and a request that you do something or be different. The first kind is about me; the second is about you. Speakers and listeners both need to be clear on this point. When a parent says what he or she wants, or "would like," is that the same as a demand on the child?

In one family, a mother apparently approved of her young teenage daughter getting advice about birth control. She said to her daughter as they drove to the birth control center, "I'd feel better if you would wait." When the daughter subsequently had sex with her boyfriend, all hell broke loose in the family. Mother had hoped that her wish would be heard as a demand and would have a powerful impact on her daughter. Daughter "heard" Mother's action, driving her to the clinic, as much more powerful than what "Mother would like."

Neither Mother nor daughter was clear about what she wanted. Daughter wanted sex with her boyfriend and at the same time she wanted to be the nice daughter who upsets no one. That she had ambivalence about having sex added to the confusion. Mother wanted to be the nice, understanding mother, whose daughter would not get angry with her. That she had ambivalence about her daughter having sex added to the confusion. They each wanted to play the comfortable role of being nice.

Real communication is not always "nice." People have emotions and express them. They react in ways that may make others uncomfortable, especially if the listener translates what is expressed as an attempt to mold and control.

As parents we owe our children authenticity. Anything else is not only phony but detrimental to everyone. We need to be real and believable. Our words and our music must go together. What we say must be borne out by how we are and what we do. We do not become authentic by learning the "skills of communication." Our authenticity shines forth when we are simply who we are. Since we are not always "nice," what we communicate won't always sound "nice," or be easy to hear. Sometimes we may feel intolerant, negative, and destructive. Those attitudes are part of the human condition; as such they are genuine responses to our children, even when we love them. Like any other feelings they do not always seem rational or justifiable. One mother told me, "I tell myself I shouldn't get angry at Henry. He's too young to even know what he is doing, but I get irrational and I'm afraid of what I might do to him."

The actions generated from our negative attitudes are potentially hurtful to a child, physically and emotionally. Therefore it is crucial for parents to have the maturity to assess their words and actions, to be in control of themselves and not just lash out at a child. To temper your expression or your actions is not covering "real" with "phony." It is staying in touch with yourself, your child, and your present situation, and acting in a nondestructive manner. Some parents are capable of this most of the time. Then there are those other times when we cannot "get hold of ourselves."

The subjects of authenticity and losing control demand another look at introjections and projections; it is through those internal gymnastics that we lose touch with ourselves and our children. When we are not in touch, there is no way we can communicate authentically.

It does not "just happen" that those who were abused as children are more likely to abuse their own children. Nor does it "just happen" that abused children are more likely to abuse their old and dependent parents. When we are young, we internalize our parents. The negative aspects that we take on are called the "introjected parent." We prefer to think we are free of those negative qualities that we so disliked in our parents. People say repeatedly and with vehemence, "I don't want to be like my mother." "I don't want to be like my father." We deny those negative qualities; they have nothing to do with us. But whatever we do not acknowledge as part of us seems to acquire a life and force of its own. Then when we are provoked we become what we hate. We are possessed. We explode, out of control; or we run on automatic, emanating the same destructive and painful tactics our parents used on us. "You'll never amount to anything." "Who do you think you are?" Perhaps we take in the cold, rejecting parent. We turn away and ignore our children, demolish them with the silent and incontestable message that they do not matter; they have no impact on us.

When these introjects, these "ghosts" take over, we lose touch with ourselves. In addition, our projections keep us out of touch with our children—and our partner. We cannot respond to others if we hear and see only what we are projecting out. Our projections are composed of the thoughts, feelings, and qualities that were unacceptable to our parents when we were young, that we "got rid of" in order to be good and lovable; the "not me." We chopped away at ourselves, disowning feelings, denying thoughts, becoming unaware of qualities we possessed, in spite of ourselves. Our children, then, are delegated to carry these unwanted parts of us that we project on them. You may experience that you make good contact with one child while another pushes all your buttons. You can be fairly certain that the "difficult" child prompts you to recall some of your own struggles from long ago.

If you experience times when you "can't get hold of yourself," gripped by some old, unfinished situation from your own childhood, possessed by ghosts of your parents, then it is especially important that you make some changes inside of you. The first step is to bring out into the daylight what has been hiding in the shadows. Open yourself to your experience—without making negative judgments about yourself. Your feelings are neither good nor bad in and of themselves, so allow yourself to get in touch. You do not need to analyze or figure out why you feel any certain way, although that is a great temptation for most of us. Simply let what you feel come into your consciousness. You may feel hesitant and stop your explorations temporarily. Be patient with yourself.

Talk to someone you trust. You may feel frightened, since many of our unfinished situations revolve around painful episodes from childhood. Unload some of the old baggage. It will be a loss you won't regret. Face the emotion-laden secrets that pull and push you. It may be the greatest gift you can give to your children, and to yourself. When you face your vintage difficulties, your "difficult" child may become easier.

Children will provoke parents. Of that we can be certain. Not because they are bad or out to get us, but simply because they are who they are, doing what they need to do in relation to the world and their family. Next time, take a look at your child and listen to him or her. Stop long enough to do that. Come to the present moment and thereby loosen the hold of the invalid apprehension, the out-of-control fear that is always the result of an instantaneous shift into the past or the future. Authentic communication requires that we get in touch with right now.

Actions generated by our response *to our child in the moment* are vastly different from those issuing from the internalized negative parent. We invariably feel a healthy identification with our child, some care, some empathy if we stay in the moment. Too much identification and we lose our boundaries; we return to the past, reliving the helplessness and fear of our early years. Too little and we become our angry, impatient, uncontrollable parent, overcome by fears of unknown possible catastrophes in the future. ("He'll never learn his lesson." "She'll get pregnant." "He'll always be a liar.") See and hear your child; take a breath and feel yourself. Dealing in the *now* opens the way for authentic response, for communication.

There is no magic. There is no perfection. The change to contact takes time. Yet at each interaction the difference may be profound. When Mom or Dad is looking daggers at the child and speaking in a louder than usual voice, the youngster might say, "You're really mad at me." "I am mad. You're right," comes the *authentic* response. That validates the child's experience. It does not mean that the parent is no longer mad, only that everyone is clear about what is taking place. Contrast that with the response, "No, I'm not mad. I don't get mad at something like this." How can a child fathom what is going on when what he perceives is denied by those he has to trust?

In addition, it is catching. One day, one of my sons asked me something about myself. My first reaction was to avoid answering. Then I said to him, "No, that's not really the way it was. This is what happened." Immediately after I stopped talking, he launched into a report of a pleasant interchange at his girlfriend's house the evening before with her folks. It had nothing to do with what I had said. It was a bit of his life that he chose to share with me—at that moment. It seemed I was given an immediate reward. One authentic response opened the way for communication, for a precious (to a mother) glimpse into his life.

Parents are too often afraid that if they reveal their human fallibility they will lose some of the authority and power of their role. Our actual power comes in the full and fragile moments when we connect person to person with the members of our family.

9 | The Toughest Job in the World

The evil we do in our family damages and distorts all members of the family—the parents who are less than they might be and the children who are less than they might be. The children grow up to become adults who are less than they might be, living lives with more pain and suffering than need be. That the evil is innocent does not make it benign.

None of us intentionally wants to foist our problems on our children. To avoid doing so means not that we have to solve all of our problems, or completely undo our childhoods or redo our parents. Rather it is up to us to discard our innocence, the innocence that keeps us bound to the old, destructive patterns, the innocence that keeps us guilty of using our children for our emotional needs. It is up to us to uncover the reality of what we are actually doing, what we are actually feeling, and what we actually need in relation to our children. The real peril resides in that which we conceal.

The most encouraging news is that when you do with intention and awareness what you are already doing—the repetitive interaction that you do unconsciously—the family changes. An example is the bickering family described earlier. When the mother openly invited the boys to carry on at the table as they normally did, the result was that they stopped their usual bickering. *The repetitive and destructive family dance can only be enacted in the dark*. It is difficult to repeat once you illuminate and recognize the dance.

For parents, married or single, taking a look at ourselves is perhaps our most crucial task. It is difficult. We are not accustomed to paying attention to questions such as those in Chapter 7. Nor have we learned to communicate as family members must in order to keep in good contact with ourselves and with one another, as discussed in Chapter 8.

We all possess important information about ourselves, inklings we hesitate to let bubble up to the surface, insights we want to avoid, intuitions we prefer not to acknowledge. The parent internalized deep inside would surely disapprove, so we must pretend, and on occasion think, "How I hate to admit it to myself, but . . ." Where does this information come from that we "hate to admit" to ourselves? It comes from the stored-up experiences, thoughts, and emotions of a lifetime. We conceal from ourselves in fear of harsh self-disapproval. If, instead, I admit to myself that I might need help, that I am lonely, that I am not as strong as I pretend to be, or that I do not like the way I am with my child, then what? Then it is possible to avert disaster. Not the disaster of owning up—there is no disaster in self-knowledge—but the disaster of self-deception.

Whatever our internal distress, it has no way to clear itself up. It is up to us to expose it to the light, to defuse our fear, pain, guilt, or need, and thus spare our children the poisonous derivatives.

Parents usually look not to themselves to find what is wrong, or to make changes in the family, but at the child, the child who is "not right," the one who is not getting on with life as the parents think he or she ought to. We parents are so sure that the problems are the child's fault. "She's made up her mind to be the way she is." This comment was made by a mother about her daughter, who was "causing" all kinds of problems with her mother and stepfather. Then the new husband added, "She's ruining our relationship." This couple blamed the daughter for their lack of harmony. They truly believed that if the daughter "got fixed," their marriage would be straightened out.

One father told me, "When I went for my own therapy my kids' problems disappeared." In a similar vein, a couple was told by a marriage counselor after one interview that they were in a difficult marriage and counseling was definitely recommended. They chose not to continue. Five years later they related the previous counselor's advice to their new counselor, adding, "Instead we sent John [their son, who was 11 at the time of the interview with the second therapist] for individual therapy for three years." This was a costly mistake; to single John out as the problem produced no positive change in the child or the marriage.

If we attribute our problems to a child, think of all the power we give to that child! And when we say, "Fix him" to the doctor or the policeman or the teacher, we think we can go on free of any responsibility for the bad or crazy kid. We want to be left alone to continue in our somnambulistic state, paying no attention to the part we play in creating our family system, a system that in some way demands a bad or crazy kid; left alone, that is, until catastrophe strikes and we awaken with a jolt.

All around us, bewildered parents are being shaken awake, usually against their will. A woman who had closed her eyes to the problems brewing in her family told me, "Suddenly everything is going wrong. Our twenty-nine-year-old daughter hates her father." In the same breath she added, "And not only that, her marriage is breaking up."

A man of twenty-two is questioned by police after setting fire to his parents' home. He tells them, "I helped build the house and they wouldn't let me in."

Two mothers told me the same story within days of each other. They are afraid to tell their sons that they are distressed about them and want them out of the house. Both are young men in their twenties, still living at home. Educated, attractive, each seems capable of taking the next step in life out into the world, to independence and maturity. Each mother fears her son might consider suicide.

Another family is grieving because their son of twenty went into the mountains and never returned. This young fellow knew the area well, had often spent time by himself there. A party of campers had seen him, realized he was not well and offered to take him back to town, but he declined their offer and insisted on staying. He died there two days later.

Each of these families has its story, which, looked at

with hindsight, makes the outcome seem inevitable. In each of the family systems, they had come to a critical time in the life cycle. Stress had built up. The patterns of interaction had solidified. The roles had become more rigid. No one knew how to make contact with anyone else.

All of these families look normal from the outside, like your family, like my family. The destructive consequences that were a reality, or a feared reality, are shocking. The usual types of subtle destructive consequences in unhealthy family systems are not obvious to the outsider, they are difficult to see, and they bring long-lasting oppression and despair.

There were three things that influenced me to write this book. The first was finding out that families that I knew were suffering tragedies like those just mentioned. Such disasters seemed so unnecessary and so alarming. Could these things happen also in my family? I thought, There but for the grace of God go I.

The second was coming across this quotation: "Good and evil are not determined by the intercourse of people with one another, but entirely by a man's relations with himself."

Third was a book by Ernest Becker, *Escape From Evil*. As I read Becker, I made a connection between his ideas about basic motivations and family relations. In light of what he said, it seemed inevitable that parents and children would be at odds with each other! Let me elaborate a bit on these ideas.

The quotation about good and evil is from the back cover of a book by Henry Miller called *Reflections on the Maurizius Case*. The observation that what we do in relation to others has everything to do with our internal conflicts reminded me of a sentence from Martin Buber's book *The Way of Man: According to the Teaching of Hasidism:* "A man should himself realize that conflict-situations between himself and others are nothing but the effects of conflict-situations in his own soul." I was familiar with internal conflicts, both my own and those of the people I worked with. I also was aware that the fragmented parts of the personality were the most dangerous, to ourselves and to others. What is not integrated is not acknowledged as part of oneself; it is cut off, denied—and powerfully destructive.

When we deny fragments of ourself we are constantly performing mental tricks. We say one thing and mean something else. We do one thing and claim we are doing something else. The internalized parent, discussed earlier, is most powerful when it is most completely denied. Whether we disown our demon of destruction, our needy child, or our grief-ridden teenager, whether we deny our sexuality, tenderness, or rage, the fragmented part will not stay dormant but will sneak out, slyly doing damage, pretending not to exist at all, or it will strike out with uncontrollable force.

The third influence I mentioned was Ernest Becker, a distinguished social theorist. He proposed that there are two basic motivations that influence everything we do: the drive for self-expansion and the need for immortality. These influences, he theorized, permeate our lives and are reflected in our behavior with others, as well as in our relations with ourselves; that is, how we talk to ourselves, drive ourselves, judge ourselves, and so on. The first of the two basic motivations is the desire to eat, grow, live, and move out into the world. Becker includes triumph over others on this list, and we might add all of those activities that involve surpassing physical human limits, such as inventing and using tools: telescopes, microphones, spaceships. As our children move out into the world, meet and embrace new ideas, take on new friends and values, they are engaging in expanding themselves and their horizons.

At each stage of growth, at every expanded horizon for the child, will the parent feel pride, and encourage the growth of independence and freedom? Or will he or she be threatened? The intensity of parents' reactions against children's steps toward independence seems to support the second basic motivation as stated by Becker: the motivation to triumph over death. He writes that all through history mankind has conceived of ways to gain immortality. Among some people it was believed that proper regard for the gods or the ancestors would guarantee life after death. Identifying with the right hero, king, or the right side, obeying certain rules of conduct have all been seen as paths to immortality. Becker goes on to say that we feel at a deep level if we hold the right beliefs, values, and ideas, we are assured that in some form we will continue to exist after death. We do, after all, kill each other over ideas. Could it be that when our beliefs and values are threatened, our chance to "sit at the right hand of God" is also threatened?

I have already mentioned the importance of safety to parents and the tragic scenes that are enacted in families when children show signs of becoming independent of their parents' authority. A young mother told me that when her parents heard that she had no intention of baptizing her daughter, their first grandchild, they offered to baby-sit for a weekend. While the parents were away they had the child baptized. The parents of the baby were incensed that the grandparents would do this against their express will. The grandparents, motivated by feelings they perhaps did not understand, did what they felt they had to do.

Again we think about parents grieving for a son who marries out of his religion as if the son were dead. He is obviously dead for them. Would it remove parents from the ranks of the holy to admit having a son who disobeys the laws, turns away from the "right way"? Does their own survival depend on disowning such an offspring? It would seem so. What power is so strong that it tears families apart, keeps countrymen pitted against one another for decades? Becker maintains it is the intent to live forever.

Whether this is a true and complete theory of what motivates us is not the issue. Rather, it is illuminating to consider parent/child interaction in light of these ideas. We come quickly to some points where parents and children are obviously going to clash.

Much of family life has order and predictability. When parents realize the dynamics that are a normal part of the inevitable antagonism between them and their children, perhaps they can more easily handle those times. There certainly will be occasions when parents are unable to support their child's reaching out in the world, either because of danger or a different point of view. From the very beginning the child's agenda differs from the parents'. The child's prime motivation is the drive to expand the self, to embrace life with zest, to feel, to do, to become bigger, faster, louder, to have influence over others. Always more, more, more. Frequently this compelling need to grow and develop is in direct confrontation with the parents' needs. People with competing agendas have a hard time making contact with each other or understanding the other's point of view.

"A battle of wills" is how one mother characterized the situation with her daughter, not yet three. How sad. How unfortunate for both of them. What a long fight they are embarking on. Could this mother be *with* the child in her daily quest to growth and still be in charge? Could she nurture and celebrate each victorious step of her child· and remain in the position of authority? Or is her fear of losing control over the child too great?

The next question is, What does the mother gain from the battle of wills? I think it a safe assumption that what appears as disobedience is often obedience. A three-year-old who is, by her mother's definition, in a battle of wills is getting an implicit message from her mother, an invitation to behave as she is behaving. Is the mother/child battle of wills a metaphor for what goes on between the parents? Granted the young one's agenda is frequently in opposition to the adults'. Yet many parents remain in charge, steering their children safely through the "terrible twos," when "no" is the favorite word, and do not experience a battle of wills.

Whenever your child seems chronically disobedient in any particular area, you would do well to look to yourself. How are you inviting this behavior? How is the family reinforcing exactly what they seem to be fighting? How is the "misbehavior" a metaphor for what is going on in the family system? Are you communicating "yes" when you believe you are saying "no," and suggesting "do" when you think you are saying "don't"?

Many examples have been given in previous chapters of subtle cues that are obeyed by children. Remember that what looks like disobedience may well be compliance.

A parent's honesty with himself or herself allows a child to simply grow up, as all children are eager to do. Otherwise they redirect their tremendous impulse to be and become into aggression, withdrawal, getting sick, being self-destructive, or developing phobias.

If you once look at your child's "bad" or "crazy" behavior, or the difficult interaction between you and your child, as the product of your own hidden needs and desires—even if it seems irrational and senseless to you—then you will have made an invaluable move away from mythology toward reality, away from dealing with a narcissistic projection toward authentic interaction with the child.

Every parent eventually learns that nagging and threats accomplish little, if anything, in changing anyone's behavior. Yet we senselessly continue what does not work, even intensify what has been unsuccessful, believing if we do it more, harder, louder, angrier, we will succeed. Not so. Therefore, looking at yourself and your family system is a fruitful alternative. As soon as you do, "fault" and "blame," "bad" and "crazy" become irrelevant. You are not waiting, helpless, for your child to change, to do something different; instead *you* do something different inside and out.

An illustration is the case of William, who was slow, slow, slow—at home, at school, everywhere. The whole family expected that William would be slow, yet they all nagged and threatened to no avail. One day, with the help of a therapist, William's mother experienced a subtle internal shift. Her attitude changed, which subsequently showed up in her approach. One day, she said to William: "Be sure you take all the time you need for your homework. I know how important it is for you to do it well." She also praised him when he finished. Immediately there was a remarkable change, at home and at school. William's mother said, "It is such a relief not to be always on his case." The family system was healthy and flexible enough to change. William was released from the role of "slow one" and the other members were released from their repetitive and rigid interaction centering around William, through which they had reinforced what they all hated.

Our ways of reinforcing the roles our children take are often subtle and unintentional. I am reminded of two birthday cards that a grandmother chose for two of her grandsons in separate families on their fourteenth birthdays, only days apart. To one she sent a picture of a person happily working in a workshop. The card said, "Life is like fresh lumber—you're always building something wonderful with it." To the second grandson went a picture of a hunter with a glint in his eye, in a jungle, a snake in the grass, and behind him, a benign-looking lion. "Hope your birthday is wild and wonderful."

In families where there is a chronic battle of wills the only alternatives are to win, lose, or draw. One may appear to win but it is a hollow victory, for when the other loses everyone else in the family system loses. Lingering pain in any member infects the others. A draw means gradual loss of contact and increasing alienation. However, a complete aboutface (as in the case of William's mother) positions you alongside your child and invites more productive alternatives for both of you.

The story of William exemplifies a fundamental change for his family. This is possible in all of our families when we take the step of paying attention to ourselves. We discover options. We have choices. We can make changes in ourselves and facilitate changes in our family system. Once you alter how you look at what is going on and how you experience the interaction in the family, your attitude shifts and you respond differently to your family situation. What is more, you will know from your experience that you can act as a responsible adult, that you do not have to be taken over by automatic, repetitive interaction. No matter how insignificant a single measure may seem, with each step you find you have the capability to engage in the process of healthier interaction. And you can do it again. Each time it is easier. To get off "automatic" and truly to engage requires some energy and some investment to avoid the habitual and the unproductive. The splendid payoff is an atmosphere in which everyone in the family can bloom.

Sometimes the family situation becomes so confused, so snarled, that you need help. Then you may decide to go for a family check-up. The family is certainly as important as your car. Take advantage of one of the many excellently trained family counselors and therapists, who know how to help your family move in a happier direction.

Parents need some time and space for themselves. We need to feel we are decent people and adequate parents, even though we may not be perfect, whatever that is! We need, in differing degrees, emotional safety. We need our lives to have meaning, and to escape the insignificance and vulnerability that the individual experiences alone in the universe as he or she faces death. *Our children are not here to supply all we need.*

A study by Burton White shows that in bringing up healthy, creative, and self-assured youngsters, the amount of time and money spent by parents is not the important thing. What matters is how the parents themselves are in life. Most significant in successful parenting is that parents feel good about their own lives, that they serve as resources for their children, and that they give them the emotional space necessary to become what they may be. *That parents feel good about their own lives* is number one in significance.

Parents who feel good about themselves have no need to work out their problems and ambitions on their youngsters. They are able to keep the boundaries clear between what they need for themselves and what their children need from them. They can separate their children's fears and frustrations from their own. Clarity leads the way for good contact and direct communication.

Communication skills are not hard to learn. What is much more difficult is to integrate feelings into the process of family communication. Exclude feelings and you exclude the people; instead you get roles. Exclude feelings and nothing changes in your system. But include feelings and the result is a kind of alchemy. Self-disclosure transmutes alienation into connection. When you and your children talk about yourselves, you admit you are human and genuinely become more so in the process. When you talk about your dreams and your fears, when you share your thoughts and your feelings, you step out of roles and become people to one another. If you have never done that together, or if you have built up walls and feel little connection and want to do something about the situation, then that is where to start.

As parents you need to take the first step. If your intention is to get in touch with your child, that will come through, not merely by asking questions but by talking about yourself, how you are in the moment. If you are *with* your child, that will come through, too. Are you unsure? Are you excited? Are you afraid? If your intention is partially to get in touch and partially to reform, control, or teach a lesson—or make your child your confidant—then that will also come through and your child will pick it up. We cannot expect our children to trust us when we are fragmented, when we have a hidden agenda for ourselves and for them.

When my oldest child was about six months old, I was in my parents' kitchen doing the dishes with my aunt, who was also visiting there. I remember that she said she had recently had new wallpaper hung in her bedroom and had not put her children's pictures back on the walls. "Those baby pictures have nothing to do with my children now," she said. Her children at that time must have been in their forties and fifties. That statement made quite an impression on me. Would I ever feel like that? I could not imagine it. Nor could I understand the innumerable older women who said to me, "Enjoy them now. They grow up so fast."

My aunt and my mother exchanged a few words about parenting. Whether it was for my benefit I cannot say. I was only twenty-one and had many years of bringing up children ahead of me. Their comments seemed important to me at that time. My mother said, "Never do anything for your children expecting gratitude." There was no disappointment in her voice, no suggestion of "poor me." I have thought of her remark many times and appreciated the wisdom of it. To expect gratitude from our children is another variety of hidden agenda. As soon as we expect something in return for what we do for our children we are setting up a bargain, striking a deal: I'll do this for you and you do that for me. We will surely end up disappointed. They are not party to any deals. Children take what we give as their due.

Acts of caring, acts of love, are simply that. They are central to all of our parenting. We are given no guarantees that our children will be grateful, or appreciate us, or think of us as good parents.

This book has dealt with the unintentional evil we do in our families. Every quality is defined by its opposite, and the opposite of evil is good. Genuine acts of parental caring and loving, whether it is comforting a fretful infant or setting limits for a rambunctious teenager, feel good and they *are* good. They are beneficial to our children, and no less beneficial to us, the parents. What, after all, is most meaningful in life? Our precious connections with those we love. As we interact with our children, whether infants, toddlers, teenagers, or adults, we have countless opportunities to create a relationship, to create an atmosphere that fosters the total well-being of another; not just any other, but this most special person we have welcomed into the world, our child.

Our satisfactions come not at some end point down the road when our child may say, "Thanks, you were great." They are inherent in the moments of loving and caring, when we are realizing the most difficult task in the world, being a parent.